365 DAYS OF SMOOTHIE RECIPES

EMMA KATIE

Copyright © 2016 Emma Katie

All rights reserved.

This book is licensed for your personal enjoyment only. This book may not be re-sold or given away to other people. If you would like to share this book with another person, please purchase an additional copy for each recipient. If you're reading this book and did not purchase it, or it was not purchased for your enjoyment only, then please return to your favorite retailer and purchase your own copy. Thank you for respecting the hard work of this author.

No part of this book may be reproduced in any form or by any electronic or mechanical means, including information storage and retrieval systems, without written permission from the author, except for the use of brief quotations in a book review. If you would like to use material from the book (other than just simply for reviewing the book), prior permission must be obtained by contacting the author at emma.katie@outlook.com.

Check out more books by Emma Katie at:
www.amazon.com/author/emmakatie

Contents

Introduction xiii
Advantages of Drinking Smoothies xiv

365 days of Smoothie Recipes

Banana Oat Smoothie 1
Hearty Fruit & Oat Smoothie 1
Refreshing Mango Orange Smoothie 1
Grapefruit Strawberry Smoothie 2
Avocado Smoothie with Vanilla 2
Tofu and Berries Smoothie 2
Ever Youth Smoothie 3
Soy Milk Smoothie 3
Tofu and Tea Smoothie 3
Banana and Buttermilk Smoothie 4
Orange and Berries Smoothie 4
Peach and Orange Smoothie 4
Avocado and Mango Smoothie 5
Banana Smoothie with Oats 5
Pineapple Smoothie with Ginger 5
Mango and Carrot Smoothie 6
Strawberry and Banana Smoothie with Tofu 6
Papaya Smoothie with Ginger 6
Pear and Yoghurt Smoothie 7
Blueberry and Banana Smoothie 7
Blackberry Smoothie with Yoghurt 7
Cranberry Protein Smoothie 8
Vanilla and Plum Smoothie 8
Carrot and Apple Smoothie with Ginger 8
Pear and Avocado Smoothie 9
Peach with Almond Butter Smoothie 9
Honey Avocado Smoothie 10
Pineapple and Kale Smoothie 10
Pumpkin and Banana Smoothie 10
Chilled Pomegranate and Blueberry Smoothie 11
Chocolate Smoothie with Peanut Butter 11
Watermelon and Mint Smoothie 11
Beets and Mixed Berries Smoothie 12
Tangy Oats and Banana Smoothie 12

Caramel and Tofu Smoothie..12
Green Tea with Kiwi Smoothie..13
Mixed Berries with Spinach Smoothie 13
Green Tea Smoothie with Avocado 13
Pineapple and Kiwi Smoothie 14
Passion Fruit Smoothie..14
Soy Milk and Espresso Smoothie 14
Apple and Blackberry Smoothie15
Veggie Smoothie 15
Mixed Berries and Apple Smoothie 15
Vanilla Peach Smoothie 16
Banana and Agave Nectar Smoothie..16
Cool Mint and Cucumber Smoothie 16
Mango Smoothie with Peach...17
Tofu Blackberry Smoothie with Walnuts 17
Vanilla and Peanut Butter Smoothie 17
Pineapple Yoghurt Smoothie...18
Kiwi Soy Milk Smoothie 18
Mango Lime Smoothie..18
Orange Cinnamon Smoothie 19
Energizing Blueberry Smoothie...19
Sweet Cherries Smoothie 19
Orange-Berries Smoothie 20
Mango Sunshine Smoothie 20
Oatmeal Smoothie with Strawberry...20
Melon and Kiwi Smoothie 21
Lean Green Smoothie 21
Mango Vanilla Smoothie...21
Rehydrating Watermelon Smoothie 22
Spiced Banana Smoothie...22
Tangy Berry Smoothie 22
Honeydew Mint Smoothie 23
Peanut Butter and Banana Smoothie..23
Cocoa and Banana Smoothie 23
Cherry and Chocolate Smoothie 24
Mixed Berries and Cereal Smoothie 24
Raspberry Vanilla Smoothie..24
Blueberry with Soy Milk Smoothie 25
Cocoa and Avocado Smoothie 25
Salad Smoothie 25
Spinach and Banana Smoothie...26
Oatmeal and Apple Smoothie 26
Spicy Peach Smoothie 26

Grapes and Peanut Butter Smoothie	27
Carrot and Apple Smoothie	27
Kale with Fruits Smoothie	27
Melon and Cucumber Smoothie	28
Pear and Orange Smoothie	28
Cereals and Cinnamon Smoothie	28
Strawberry Smoothie with Orange	29
Vanilla Pumpkin Smoothie	29
Grapefruit and Mixed Berries Smoothie	29
Pineapple- Orange Smoothie	30
Green Morning Smoothie	30
Orange Vanilla Smoothie	30
Mango Smoothie with Mint	31
Healthy Kefir Smoothie	31
Apple Smoothie with Peanut Butter	31
Creamy Chocolate Milk Smoothie	32
Sweet Potato Smoothie with Peach	32
Plum Yoghurt Smoothie	32
Pineapple Vanilla Smoothie	33
Milky Banana Smoothie	33
Creamy Banana Smoothie	33
Honey Blackberries Smoothie	34
Guava Smoothie with Strawberry	34
Cucumber Tomato Smoothie	34
Grape and Raspberry Smoothie	35
Chocolate Cinnamon Smoothie	35
Coconut and Lime Smoothie	35
Mixed Berries and Oats Smoothie	36
Refreshing Berry Orange Smoothie	36
Pineapple with Almond Milk Smoothie	36
Green Tea and Melon Smoothie	37
Pineapple Smoothie with Coconut	37
Green Tea and Blueberry Smoothie	37
Mango Coconut Smoothie	38
Chocolate and Cherry Smoothie	38
Blueberry Smoothie with Almond Butter	38
Go Green Smoothie	39
Chilled Pomegranate and Berry Smoothie	39
Blueberry and Kiwi Smoothie	39
Banana and Greens Smoothie	40
Tofu Smoothie with Fruits	40
Cinnamon and Berries Smoothie	40
Oats and Ginger Berry Smoothie	41

Creamy Cashew Smoothie	41
Blueberry Smoothie with Flax Seeds	41
Mango and Yoghurt Smoothie	42
Chamomile Banana Smoothie	42
Banana and Coffee Smoothie	42
Strawberry Yoghurt Smoothie	43
Healthy Green Smoothie	43
Ginger Orange Smoothie	43
Buttermilk and Dates Smoothie	44
Mixed Berries Smoothie	44
Soy Milk and Strawberry Smoothie	44
Antioxidant Pomegranate Smoothie	45
Carrot and Red Beet Smoothie	45
Wheat Germ and Blackberry Smoothie	45
Apple Ginger and Carrot Smoothie	46
Cucumber and Melon Smoothie	46
Banana Smoothie with Peanut Butter	46
Mango and Carrot Smoothie with Herbs	47
Pure Vegan Smoothie	47
Slushy Orange Smoothie	47
Clean Breeze Smoothie	48
Creamsicle Breakfast Smoothie	48
Citrus Berry Smoothie	48
Coffee-Banana Tofu Shake	49
Spiced Banana Smoothie	49
Strawberry Smoothie	49
Apricot Smoothie	50
Green Tea Smoothie	50
Tropical Fruit Smoothie	50
Banana-Berry Smoothie	51
Melon-Ginger Smoothie	51
Apricot Smoothie	51
Pomegranate Berries Smoothie	52
Raspberry-Avocado Smoothie	52
Citrus Berries Smoothie	52
Thermos-Ready Smoothie	53
Tropical Tofu Smoothie	53
Tropical Fruit Smoothie	53
Wake-Up Smoothie	54
Banana-Berry Smoothie	54
Banana-Cocoa Soy Smoothie	54
Banana Liven Smoothie	55
Coffee-Banana Tofu Smoothie	55

Cantaloupe Smoothie	55
Clean Wind Smoothie	56
Creamsicle Smoothie	56
Fresh Fruit Vanilla Smoothie	56
Orange and Flax Seed Smoothie	56
Good Natural Tea Smoothie	57
Hawaiian Smoothie	57
Mango Lassi Smoothie	57
Melon-Ginger Smoothie	58
Pineapple-Coconut Frappe	58
Cherry Vanilla Smoothie	58
Avocado Blueberry Smoothie	58
Strawberry Oatmeal Breakfast Smoothie	59
All-Round Good Smoothie	59
Triple Berry Blend	59
Pineapple and Banana Smoothie	60
Apricot-Almond Smoothie	60
Walnut toffee and Chocolate Smoothie	60
Banana Caramel Smoothie	61
Green Envy Avocado Smoothie	61
Peppermint smoothie	61
Broccoli and Spinach Smoothie	62
Ginger Coconut Smoothie	62
Plum and Blueberry Smoothie	62
Carrot-Apple Smoothie	62
Kiwi-Strawberry Smoothie	63
Cherry-Vanilla smoothie	63
Apple and Oats Smoothie	63
Pineapple and Mango Smoothie	64
Banana Crunch Smoothie	64
Pineapple and Banana Smoothie	64
Healthy Berry Smoothie	65
No-fat Fruit Smoothie	65
Raspberry Lime Smoothie	65
Tropical Berry Tofu Smoothie	66
Banana Orange Smoothie	66
Yogurt Fruit Smoothie	66
Raspberry Strawberry Smoothie	66
Strawberry Blueberry and Banana Smoothie	67
Blueberry Acai Berry Smoothie	67
Purple Detox Smoothie	67
Blueberry Banana Smoothie, with Fax Seeds	68
Gluten-Free Berry Smoothie	68

- Chocolate Banana smoothie 68
- Healthy Heart Smoothie 69
- Wheat Germ Smoothie 69
- Sunup Smoothie 69
- Protein Rich smoothie 69
- Low Carb Smoothie 70
- Chocolate and Peanut butter- Banana Smoothie 70
- Peanut Butter and Oatmeal Smoothie 70
- Orange and Melon Smoothie 71
- Tomato Smoothie 71
- Watermelon and Strawberry Smoothie 71
- Limey Watermelon Smoothie 72
- Cherry Cantaloupe Smoothie 72
- Berry Healthy Smoothie Recipe 72
- Classic Green Detox Smoothie With Kale 72
- Simple Smoothie Detox 73
- Rise and Shine Smoothie 73
- Ruby Red Grapefruit Smoothie 73
- Cherry Lemon Buzz Smoothie 74
- Protein Power Smoothie 74
- Heart Healthy Oats and Fruit Smoothie 74
- Berry Banana smoothie 74
- Blackberry and Peach Smoothie 75
- Berry Fruit Smoothies 75
- Green Smoothie 75
- Sunrise Smoothies 76
- Orange Creamsicle Smoothies 76
- Strawberry Smoothie 76
- Berry Blast Smoothie 77
- Pineapple Coconut Smoothie 77
- Banana Smoothie 77
- Watermelon Smoothie 78
- Chocolate Banana Smoothie 78
- Blueberry Fruit Smoothies 78
- Peach Smoothie 78
- Chocolate Strawberry Smoothies 79
- Pumpkin Smoothies 79
- Mixed fruit Smoothie 79
- Pomegranate Berry Smoothie 80
- Cantaloupe Smoothie 80
- PB&J Smoothie 80
- Tropical Morning Smoothie 80
- Honeydew-Kiwifruit Smoothie 81

Title	Page
Apple Sangria Smoothie	81
Pomegranate Berry Smoothie	81
Cantaloupe Smoothie	82
Green Smoothie with Kefir	82
Green Smoothie with Spinach Banana Berries	82
Freckled PB&J	83
Berry Good Smoothie	83
Frog Juice Smoothie	83
Peanut Butter Cup Smoothie	83
Blueberry Cheesecake Smoothie	84
Tea for Two Smoothie	84
Apple Crisp Smoothie	84
Cream Smoothie	84
Avocado-Pear Smoothie	85
Banana and Kiwi Smoothie	85
Yogurt-Pistachio Smoothies	85
Fruit Smoothie	86
Strawberry, Mango, and Yogurt Smoothie	86
Banana, Oat and Fig Smoothie	86
Creamy Date Smoothie	86
Banana Apricot and Mango smoothie	87
Banana and Strawberry Smoothies	87
Spiced Pumpkin Smoothie	87
Banana and Berry Smoothie	88
Peach, Pear and Fresh Ginger Smoothies	88
Strawberry and Mango Smoothie	88
Collard Green Lime and Mango Smoothie	89
Raspberry and Peach Smoothie	89
Orange - Cranberry Power Smoothie	89
Chocolate Strawberry Smoothie	90
Banana and Peanut smoothie	90
Blackberries Smoothie with Strawberries Toppings	90
Kiwi Orange Smoothie	91
Strawberry Smoothie with Watermelon	91
Neem-Lemon Smoothie	91
Fresh Cream Fruit Smoothie	92
Green Mango Pepper Smoothie Ingredients	92
Protein Enriched Strawberry Smoothie	92
Blueberry Peppermint Smoothie	93
Vodka-Cream Smoothie	93
Carrot Smoothie	93
Chocolate Cookies with Ice- cream Smoothie	94
Banana-Chocolate Smoothie	94

Rainy day smoothie 94
Coolers Smoothie Ingredients 95
Pumpkin Smoothie 95
Caramel Smoothie 95
Sweet Spinach Smoothie 96
Pineapple Smoothie 96
Asparagus Smoothie 96
Deep Blue Smoothie 97
Yogurt Smoothie 97
Apricot Delight 98
Cappuccino Smoothie 98
Corn-Oats and Barley Trio 98
Cabbage smoothie 99
Golden Sun Smoothie 99
Guava Smoothie 99
Litchi Smoothie 100
Raspberry Smoothie 100
Green Envy 100
Vegan Smoothie 101
Brazilian Ginseng and Orange Smoothie 101
Cool and exotic smoothie with cucumber and mint 101
Dried Berry Smoothie 102
Lemon and Yogurt Smoothie 102
Lentil-Cashew nut Smoothie 102
Avocado Rose Smoothie 103
Pink Delight 103
Pomegranate-Chocolate Smoothie 103
Turmeric Yogurt Smoothie 104
Yogurt Beetroot Smoothie 104
Triple Delight Smoothie 104
Mixed Fruit Smoothie 105
Custard apple Smoothie 105
Espresso Smoothie with Cream and Chocolate 105
Sizzling Smoothie 106
Multicoloured Smoothie 106
Yellow Sunshine Smoothie 106
Health Smoothie Ingredients 107
Biscuit Smoothie 107
Potato Baby-corn Smoothie 107
Hale and Hearty Ginger-Banana Smoothie 108
Kiwi and strawberry smoothie 108
Avocado Smoothie 108
Raspberry Smoothies 109

Basil Smoothie 109
Banana - Papaya Smoothie 109
Pumpkin Smoothie 110
Mango Smoothie 110
Summer Day Smoothie 110
Raspberry Vanilla Smoothie 111
Purple Grape Smoothie 111
Smoothie with Berries 111
Melon Smoothie 112
Blueberry Smoothie 112
Vanilla Coconut Smoothie 112
Fresh Morning Smoothie 113
Fruit and Spice Smoothie 113
Spiced Cream n' Pumpkin Smoothie 113
Banana-Almond Milk Smoothie 114
Peanut Butter and Fruit Jelly Smoothie114
Banana- Ginger Smoothie 114
Orange-Nutmeg Dream Creamsicle 115
Green Tea and Banana Berry Smoothie 115
Dry Fruit Smoothie 115
Pineapple Passion Smoothie 116
Valentine's Smoothie 116
Cucumber Smoothie 116
Tomato-Basil Smoothie 117
Tropical Fusion Smoothie 117
Peach Smoothie 117
Tutti-Fruity Smoothie 118
Banana-Soy Smoothie 118
Carrot-Celery Smoothie 118
Rose Smoothie 119
Marshmallow Smoothie 119
Evil- Eye Smoothie 119
Bottle Gourd Smoothie 120
Cherry-Lime-Basil Smoothie 120
Ginger-Apple Smoothie 120
Raspberry-Rosemary Smoothie 121
Cilantro Smoothie 121
Raw Mango Smoothie 121
Veggie-Delight Smoothie 122
Custard- apple Smoothie 122
Cranberry Smoothie 122
Sapodilla- Coco Smoothie 123

Conclusion **125**

Introduction

Thank you for downloading the book, "365 Days of Smoothie Recipes"

There's always a smoothie for everyone, but what if we tell you that you can have a new flavor each day, for an entire year? Doesn't that sound exciting? That's exactly what this book is about! Moreover, if you're on a diet, then, you no long need to worry about your calorie intake, if you treat yourself with the goodness of each of these smoothie recipes.

These delicious and healthy smoothie recipes make it easy to eat right with fruit, vegetables, milk, immune-boosting yogurt, and other nutritious ingredients- and they're great for those on a diet too.

Smoothies are a great source of fiber and it helps people suffering from indigestion and constipation by improving their digestive system. Since smoothies are abundant in nutrients and help recover and rebuild, the body after workouts and it is easier for the body to absorb and assimilate the nutrients in a smoothie as opposed to a meal.

Let us explore our way to good health…

Advantages of Drinking Smoothies

A smoothie is considered one of the healthiest drinks of all time. The best part about smoothies is that they are delicious and easy to make. Let's us look at some of the prime advantages of drinking smoothies.

Fruits are always good for health and smoothies contain fruit or fruit pulp as the key ingredient.

Our body needs vitamins and minerals to be fit and balanced growth. Smoothies offer essential nutrients.

Fiber is essential for digestion Smoothies are a rich source of fiber. It is easy to make smoothies. You can make smoothies in a few minutes.

365 days of Smoothie Recipes

Banana Oat Smoothie

Ingredients

¼ cup rolled oats (old –fashioned)
½ cup plain yogurt (low fat)
1 banana
½ cup milk (fat free)
¼ tsp powdered cinnamon
2 tsp honey

Preparation

Add all the ingredients carefully in a blender and blend. Gradually increase the speed from low to high. Thereafter, leave it for some time in order for the mixture to settle. Your delicious smoothie is ready. Enjoy!

Hearty Fruit & Oat Smoothie

Ingredients

1 cup strawberries
1 banana
¼ cup almonds
½ cup oats (old –fashioned)
1 tsp maple syrup
1 cup vanilla yogurt (low fat)

Preparation

Add the ingredients to the blender and blend gently. Gradually increase speed and blend for about a minute. This is an excellent, power packed smoothie for breakfast. Enjoy!

Refreshing Mango Orange Smoothie

Ingredients

1 banana, peeled and chopped
1 cup vanilla yoghurt (low fat) 1 mango, peeled and chopped
1 cup orange juice
4-5 ice cubes

Preparation

Put all the ingredients in a blender and blend them till they are smooth and frothy. You must adjust the speed of the blender from low to high. Add some ice cubes and blend it again. Your smoothie is ready. This is a perfect smoothie to start your day. Enjoy!

Grapefruit Strawberry Smoothie

Ingredients

1 grapefruit, peeled de-seeded and chopped
2 cups strawberries (frozen)
1 inch ginger, fine chopped
1 apple, peeled and chopped
1 cup water

Preparation

Combine apple, ginger, grapefruit and strawberries in a blending jar. Pour cup water and blend till all the ingredients are smooth. You may try this smoothie for your breakfast or carry it on the go. Enjoy!

Avocado Smoothie with Vanilla

Ingredients

1 avocado (ripe)
1 tsp vanilla extract
1 cup pear- nectar (without sugar)
1 cup ice cubes

Preparation

Combine ripe avocado, vanilla extract and pear- nectar in a blending jar. Blend till the ingredients are pureed. If the smoothie seems to be very thick, add some pear- nectar and adjust the consistency of your smoothie. Add the ice cubes and blend thoroughly. Serve this smoothie as breakfast. Enjoy!

Tofu and Berries Smoothie

Ingredients

¼ cup pomegranate juice
3 tsp honey
1 cup silken tofu
2 tsp flax seed (powered)
1 tsp ginger grated
2 cups mixed berries (frozen)

Preparation

Take a blending jar, add pomegranate juice, silken tofu, honey, powered flaxseed, grated ginger and mixed berries to it. Now blend thoroughly until all the ingredients are pureed well. The speed of your blender must rise from low to high. You can have this smoothie for breakfast. Enjoy!

Ever Youth Smoothie

Ingredients

½ cup organic blueberries (frozen)
½ cup green tea (chilled and unsweetened)
¾ cup organic yoghurt (low fat)
2 tsp of powered flax seed
½ cup organic strawberries (frozen)
2 tsp of honey

Preparation

Combine blueberries, strawberries, green tea, yoghurt and green tea in an electronic blending jar. Blend for 20 seconds. Add honey and blend again till smooth. Serve this smoothie for breakfast. Enjoy!

Soy Milk Smoothie

Ingredients

½ cup banana
¼ cup carrot juice
½ cup orange juice
1-2 tsp honey
½ cup pineapple, cubes
½ cup raspberries (frozen)
½ cup soy milk (vanilla)

Preparation

Blend pineapple cubes, raspberries, soy milk, orange juice, banana and carrot juice in a blending jar. Blend until all the ingredients are pureed. You must serve this smoothie immediately after preparing it. You may have this smoothie for your breakfast or have it on the go. Enjoy!

Tofu and Tea Smoothie

Ingredients

2 bags of Rooibos tea
6 ounce of silken tofu
1 cup grapes (frozen)
2 cups of sweet cherries (frozen)
½ cup blueberries (frozen)
¾ cup water

Preparation

Simmer water and remove it from flame. Now add the tea bags and let it rest for 8 minutes. Do not cover. Now remove the tea bags and put the tea in your refrigerator for cooling. Take a blending jar and add silken tofu, frozen grapes, sweet cherries, blueberries, tea in it. Blend till smooth. Enjoy!

Banana and Buttermilk Smoothie

Ingredients
10 dried dates
1 cup buttermilk (low fat)
2 bananas
2 tsp honey
Pinch of salt
1 cup ice cubes

Preparation
Peel the bananas and cut into slices. Remove the seeds of the dried dates. Combine dried dates, low fat buttermilk and banana slices in a blending jar. Blend for around 30 seconds. Now add little salt, honey and ice cubes. Blend again. Serve for breakfast. Enjoy!

Orange and Berries Smoothie

Ingredients
1 banana
½ cup yoghurt (low fat)
2 navel oranges 1 cup blueberries (frozen)
1 cup raspberries (frozen)

Preparation
Peel and deseed the navel oranges. Peel the banana and cut into slices. Combine banana slices, navel oranges, frozen blueberries, frozen raspberries and low fat yoghurt in a blending jar. Blend till smooth. Adjust the speed of your blending jar from low to high. Serve immediately for your breakfast. Enjoy!

Peach and Orange Smoothie

1 pound peaches
1/3 cup orange juice
6 ounces silken tofu
1 tsp honey

Preparation
First, make an ice bath ready. Boil water in a saucepan. Add the peaches to the boiling water and keep it for 30 seconds. Now take out the peaches and put it in the ice bath. After the peaches are cool, drain the excess water. Peel and deseed the peaches. Now combine peaches, orange juice, silken tofu and honey in a blending jar. Blend till smooth. Enjoy!

Avocado and Mango Smoothie

Ingredients

1¼ cup almond milk (soy free)
¼ cup avocado
2 kale leaves
½ cup coconut water
½ cup mango (cut into cubes)
½ cup ice cubes

Preparation

Put mango chunks, avocado, kale leaves, almond milk and coconut water in a blending jar. Blend for around 30 seconds. Now add the ice cubes and blend again till smooth. Your breakfast smoothie is ready. Enjoy!

Banana Smoothie with Oats

Ingredients

1 banana (ripe)
½ cup skimmed milk
¼ cup rolled oats
2 tsp flaxseeds
½ cup yoghurt (low fat)
1 cup ice cubes

Preparation

Peel and cut the banana into slices. Add skimmed milk, banana slices, rolled oats, flaxseeds and yoghurt in a blending jar. Blend for around 30 seconds. Now add ice cubes and blend again thoroughly. Try this smoothie for breakfast. Enjoy!

Pineapple Smoothie with Ginger

Ingredients

1 cup pineapple
1 inch ginger
1 cup pineapple juice
½ cup ice cubes
⅛ tsp powered cinnamon
½ cup yoghurt (low fat)

Preparation

Cut pineapple into small pieces. Peel and mince the ginger. Combine low fat yoghurt, pineapple juice and pineapple pieces in a blending jar. Blend for 30 seconds. Now add ice and powered cinnamon to it. Blend again. Your morning breakfast is ready. Enjoy!

Mango and Carrot Smoothie

Ingredients

1 mango (peeled and chopped)
A pinch nutmeg powder
1 cup carrot juice
½ cup ice cubes

Preparation

Combine chopped mango and carrot juice in a blending jar. Blend till smooth. Now add a pinch of freshly grated nutmeg and ice and blend again till all the ingredients are mixed well. If you are using frozen mango, do not add ice to the smoothie. Serve it for breakfast or as an evening snack. Enjoy!

Strawberry and Banana Smoothie with Tofu

Ingredients

10 ounce strawberries (unsweetened)
12 ounce silken tofu
2 tsp lemon juice
¼ cup honey
1 cup soy milk
1 banana (ripe)
Salt to taste

Preparation

Peel and cut banana into pieces. Take an electronic blender and add banana pieces, soy milk, lemon juice, silken tofu, strawberries, honey and ice. Blend till smooth. Add salt to taste. Blend again. Top it with pureed strawberry (optional). Your evening snack is ready. Enjoy!

Papaya Smoothie with Ginger

Ingredients

2/3 cup yoghurt (low fat)
1 tsp ginger, grated
2 lemons (juiced)
20 mint leaves
2 ½ cup papaya chunks
1 tsp honey
1 cup ice cubes

Preparation

Add low fat yoghurt, grated ginger, lemon juice, papaya chunks and 16 mint leaves in an electronic blending jar. Blend till smooth. Add the ice cubes and blend again thoroughly. Garnish with fresh mint leaves while serving. Try this smoothie as an appetizer. Enjoy!

Pear and Yoghurt Smoothie

Ingredients
1 banana
2 tsp protein powder
½ cup pear
1 ½ low fat yoghurt
¾ cup ice cubes

Preparation
Peel the banana and pear and chop them. Take an electronic blending jar and combine banana, pear, low fat yoghurt and protein powder. Blend on high speed so that the ingredients get pureed well. Add ice cubes and give a quick blend. Make sure that the ice cubes are mixed smoothly. Your smoothie is ready. Enjoy!

Blueberry and Banana Smoothie

Ingredients
1 banana (ripe)
1 cup blueberries (frozen)
1 cup yoghurt (low fat)

Preparation
Peel and cut the banana into small pieces. Take an electronic blending jar. Add banana slices, frozen yoghurt and a cup of low fat yoghurt. Blend till all the ingredients are smoothly pureed. Adjust the speed of your blender from low to high to make the smoothie frothy. Serve this as a breakfast. Enjoy!

Blackberry Smoothie with Yoghurt

Ingredients
1 cup yoghurt (low fat)
3 cups blackberries (frozen)
1 cup buttermilk (low fat)
3-4 tsp honey
Pinch of powered cardamom

Preparation
Add low fat buttermilk, low fat yoghurt and frozen blackberries in an electronic blending jar. Blend for around 30 seconds. Add honey and freshly powered cardamom powder to the smoothie. Blend again thoroughly. Serve this as breakfast. Enjoy!

Cranberry Protein Smoothie

Give a protein boost to your body in the morning breakfast, with cranberry protein smoothie. Cranberry is rich in Vitamin C, Vitamin E and fiber. So, this smoothie is a great way to include cranberry in your diet. No sugar or sweetener is added to the smoothie. Thus, you need not worry about the calorie count while sipping this delicious and creamy smoothie. It takes 5-10 minutes to prepare this smoothie.

Ingredients
1 ¼ cup cranberry juice (without sugar)
2 scoops of protein powder (vanilla flavour)
5 ice cubes

Preparation
Use an electronic blending jar. Add two scoops of protein powder and unsweetened cranberry juice in it. Blend till the ingredients turn smooth. Add ice cubes. Blend again thoroughly. Serve this in breakfast. Enjoy!

Vanilla and Plum Smoothie

Welcome your guests with the delicious vanilla and plum smoothie. Buttermilk makes the smoothie filling and gives the desired thickness to the smoothie.

Ingredients
1 vanilla bean
½ cup buttermilk
5 plums
2 cups sugar
1 ½ cup ice cubes
4 cups of water

Preparation
Cut the vanilla bean into halves and scrape the seeds. Take 4 cups of water in a saucepan. Add vanilla bean extract and sugar and bring to boil. Keep on stirring until the sugar is dissolved. Add plums and simmer till they turn limp. Remove the plums and deseed them. Discard poaching water. Add plums, ice and buttermilk in a blending jar. Blend till they are smoothly pureed. You may serve this smoothie at any time during the day. Enjoy!

Carrot and Apple Smoothie with Ginger

It is said that an apple a day keeps doctor away. To increase the nutritional benefits, carrots are added to the smoothie. Apples and carrots have proven health benefits. Add ginger to add zing Honey is used as the sweetener which also helps you to stay fit.

Ingredients
1 green apple
1 cup carrot juice
1 cup orange juice
2 tsp ginger, grated
1 tsp honey

Preparation

Refrigerate carrot juice in an ice tray. Peel and chop the green apple. Use a blender. Add frozen carrot juice cubes, green apple, orange juice, grated ginger and honey. Blend till smooth. Enjoy!

Pear and Avocado Smoothie

Pear and avocado smoothie is a perfect option to feel refresh. Silken tofu makes the smoothie filling. Honey is used as the sweetener to keep it low on calories. Vanilla adds flavor to the smoothie. It takes a few minutes to prepare this delicious smoothie.

Ingredients

1 Hass avocado (ripe)
1 cup pear juice
½ cup silken tofu

½ tsp vanilla extract
2 cups ice
2 tsp honey

Preparation

Peel and pit the avocado. Add avocado, pear juice, silken tofu, honey and vanilla extract in an electronic blending jar. Blend till all the ingredients are pureed well. Add ice and blend again thoroughly. Your breakfast smoothie is ready to be served. Enjoy!

Peach with Almond Butter Smoothie

You may opt for peach with almond butter smoothie for both breakfast as well as dinner. Peach and almond butter with cardamom infused flavor will treat your taste buds. The smoothie is filling and energizing at the same time. Almond butter makes the smoothie rich and creamy in texture. You may prepare and preserve the smoothie for a day in refrigerator.

Ingredients

1 cup peach (frozen)
2 tsp agave syrup
1 tsp powered powdered cardamom

¼ cup almond butter
2 cups water
½ cup ice cubes

Preparation

Blend almond butter, peach, agave syrup, frozen peach and water till smooth. Add freshly powered cardamom and ice cubes and blend again thoroughly. You may serve this smoothie as breakfast or dinner. Enjoy!

Honey Avocado Smoothie

Avocado is rich in vitamins and fiber content. Thus, you must include avocado in your daily diet. Honey avocado smoothie is perfect to beat the heat in scorching summers. White creamy smoothie with honey and vanilla flavor is delicious enough to be relished by all.

Ingredients

1 cup low fat milk
4 tsp honey
½ cup vanilla yoghurt
1 avocado (ripe)
8-9 ice cubes

Preparation

The avocado must be halved as well as pitted. Add low fat milk, vanilla yoghurt, avocado and honey in a blending jar. Blend them till smooth. Add in the ice cubes and blend again. You may garnish with few mint leaves or cherries. This cooling smoothie is perfect to have with lunch. Enjoy!

Pineapple and Kale Smoothie

Ingredients

½ cup chopped kale leaves
½ cup pineapple (cut into cubes)
½ cup fresh pineapple juice
1 banana (ripe)
1 cup almond milk (unsweetened)

Preparation

Peel and cut the banana into slices. Combine banana slices, almond milk, kale leaves, almond milk, pineapple cubes and pineapple juice in a blender. Blend till all the ingredients are smoothly pureed. Serve this smoothie for breakfast. Enjoy!

Pumpkin and Banana Smoothie

Ingredients

1 cup vanilla yoghurt
¾ cup pumpkin (chilled)
1 tsp of brown sugar
1/3 cup orange juice
½ cup ice cubes
½ tsp of cinnamon (powered)
1/8 tsp of nutmeg (powered)
1 banana (frozen)
A pinch of powered cloves

Preparation

Combine vanilla yoghurt, chilled pumpkin, frozen banana, orange juice and brown sugar in a blending jar. Blend well. Now add powered cinnamon, powdered cloves and ice cubes. Blend again till smooth. You may serve this smoothie in breakfast. Enjoy!

Chilled Pomegranate and Blueberry Smoothie

Ingredients

½ cup pomegranate juice (chilled)
2 cups blueberries (frozen)

½ cup vanilla yoghurt (low fat)
Sugar- As per taste

Preparation

Add frozen mixed berries and half cup pomegranate juice in a blending jar and blend it till smooth. After blending, add low-fat vanilla yoghurt and blend it again till smooth and frothy. You may add sugar. Adjust the speed of the blended from low to high. The smoothie is perfect for your breakfast.Enjoy!

Chocolate Smoothie with Peanut Butter

Ingredients

½ cup low fat milk
2 tsp peanut butter
1 ripe banana (frozen)

8 ounces vanilla yoghurt (low fat)
2 tsp chocolate syrup

Preparation

Chop the frozen banana into slices. Blend banana slices, vanilla, peanut butter, yoghurt, chocolate syrup and milk in a blender. Blend till smooth. Adjust the speed of the smoothie from low to high. Your breakfast smoothie is ready. Enjoy!

Watermelon and Mint Smoothie

Ingredients

1/3 cup plain yoghurt (low fat)
2 cups watermelon (seedless)

2 tsp mint leaves (chopped)

Preparation

Chop watermelon into small pieces. Take the blending jar and combine low fat yoghurt, chopped mint leaves and watermelon. Blend till all the ingredients are smoothly pureed. Adjust the speed of the blender from low to high. You may use vanilla yoghurt instead of plain yoghurt. Serve this smoothie as breakfast or have it on the go. Enjoy!

Beets and Mixed Berries Smoothie

Ingredients

¼ cup orange juice
1 cup blueberries
1 tsp honey
1 cup raspberries (frozen)
1/3 cup beets (cooked)
¼ cup yoghurt (fat free)

Preparation

Combine orange juice, blueberries, blanched beets, yoghurt and raspberries in a blending jar. Blend till the ingredients are smoothly pureed. Add honey and blend again thoroughly. Your breakfast smoothie is ready in few minutes. You may also serve this smoothie in the afternoon. Enjoy!

Tangy Oats and Banana Smoothie

Ingredients

2/3 cup orange juice
1 banana (frozen)
½ cup oats (cooked)
1 tsp honey
½ cup yoghurt (low fat)
1 tsp flaxseed meal
1 cup ice cubes
½ tsp orange rind (grated)

Preparation

Cut the frozen banana into small pieces. Combine banana slices, cooked oats, orange juice, low fat yoghurt, flaxseed meal and orange in a blending jar. Blend till smoothly. Add ice cubes and blend again. Enjoy!

Caramel and Tofu Smoothie

Ingredients

¾ cup vanilla flavoured soy milk
2 tsp caramel syrup (fat free)
6 ounces of silken tofu (chilled)
1 packet of instant coffee (iced)
2 cups ice cubes

Preparation

Add soy milk, silken tofu, instant coffee and soy milk in a blending jar. Blend for 30 seconds. Add ice cubes and blend again till smooth. Your breakfast smoothie is ready. Enjoy!

Green Tea with Kiwi Smoothie

Ingredients

2 ½ cups diced mango (frozen)
2 tsp green tea
¾ cup vanilla yoghurt (fat free)
½ cup baby spinach
¼ cup honey

2 cups ice cubes
2 tsp water
3 peeled kiwifruit
½ tsp lime rind (grated)

Preparation

Blend the mango, yoghurt, ns honey, lime rind and water in a blender. Blend till smooth. Pour the liquid in a glass and cool it in refrigerator. Rinse the blending jar thoroughly. Blend rest of the ingredients. Pour the mango mixture with this green mixture. Enjoy!

Mixed Berries with Spinach Smoothie

Ingredients

1 cup fresh orange juice
1 ½ cup spinach leaves
1 cup blueberries (frozen)

1 cup raspberries (frozen)
1 cup strawberries (frozen)
2 tsp honey

Preparation

Combine orange juice, blueberries, raspberries, strawberries and spinach leaves in a blending jar. Blend at high speed till the spinach is completely pureed and. Add honey and blend till smooth. Your breakfast smoothie is ready. Enjoy!

Green Tea Smoothie with Avocado

Ingredients

1 ½ cups brewed green tea
1 avocado (ripe)
3 cups white wine grapes

2 baby spinach leaves
2 tsp honey

Preparation

Blend brewed green tea, ripe avocado, baby spinach leaves and white wine grapes in a blending jar. Blend till the ingredients are smooth. Add honey and blend again. You may serve this smoothie for breakfast. Enjoy!

365 Days of Smoothie Recipes

Pineapple and Kiwi Smoothie

Ingredients

¼ cup brewed green tea
½ cup pineapple (cut into cubes)
1 ripe banana (frozen)
1 kiwi (peeled)
4 ice cubes

Preparation

Add pineapple cubes, brewed green tea, banana and kiwi slices in a blending jar. Blend till smooth. Add ice and blend again. Serve immediately. Enjoy!

Passion Fruit Smoothie

Ingredients

1 cup yoghurt (fat free)
1 banana (ripe)
½ cup passion fruit nectar
12 ounce blueberries (frozen)
1 ½ tsp wheat germ (toasted)
2 tsp honey
½ cup ice cubes

Preparation

Take a blending jar. Combine all the ingredients. Blend thoroughly till smooth. Adjust the speed of the blender from low to high. Serve it as a snack. Enjoy!

Soy Milk and Espresso Smoothie

Ingredients

½ cup soy milk (vanilla)
1 ripe banana
1 tsp cashew butter
¼ cup chilled espresso
3-4 ice cubes

Preparation

Peel and cut the banana into thick slices. Combine chilled espresso, cashew butter, banana, and soy milk in an electronic blending jar. Blend till all the ingredients are smoothly pureed. Add ice cubes and blend again till smooth. You may serve the smoothie as an evening snack. Enjoy!

Apple and Blackberry Smoothie

Ingredients

1 apple
2 cups blackberries (frozen)
2/3 cup lemon yoghurt (low fat)
½ cup apple cider

Preparation

Cut the apple into small sized pieces. Combine frozen berries, apple, apple cider, and lemon yoghurt in an electronic blending jar. Blend well till all the ingredients are mixed smoothly. Adjust the speed of your blender from low to high. Serve this smoothie in breakfast. Enjoy!

Veggie Smoothie

Ingredients

2 cups tomato juice
½ cup red bell pepper (chopped)
3 tsp fresh lemon juice
½ cup cucumber (chopped)
2 tsp chopped scallions
¼ tsp freshly powered pepper
2 tsp Worcester sauce
¼ tsp of hot pepper sauce
¼ tsp of salt

Preparation

Add all the ingredients in a blending jar. Blend till all the ingredients are smoothly pureed. Blend for about 3 to 4 minutes adjusting the speed of your blender from low to high. Refrigerate for 30 minutes and serve as lunch smoothie. Enjoy!

Mixed Berries and Apple Smoothie

Ingredients

1 cup mixed berries (frozen)
½ cup apple juice
½ banana
¼ cup silken tofu

Preparation

Peel and cut the banana into slices. Combine banana slices, silken tofu, apple juice and frozen mixed berries in an electronic blending jar. Blend till all the ingredients are smoothly mixed. Adjust the speed of your blender from low to high to make the smoothie creamy and frothy. Your breakfast smoothie is ready. Enjoy!

Vanilla Peach Smoothie

Ingredients
3 peaches
1 tsp lemon juice
½ cup milk (low fat)
1 cup vanilla ice cream

Preparation
Peel and deseed the peaches. Cut it into cubes. Add peach cubes, fresh lemon juice, low fat milk and vanilla ice cream in a blending jar and blend till all the ingredients are pureed smoothly. Adjust the speed of your blender from low to high. Garnish the smoothie with few peach slices. Enjoy!

Banana and Agave Nectar Smoothie

Ingredients
1/3 cup thawed blueberries (frozen)
2 tsp of agave nectar (light in color)
1 banana (chilled)
1 cup yoghurt (fat free)

Preparation
Peel and slice the banana. Combine low fat yoghurt, banana slices, agave nectar and frozen blueberries in a blending jar. Blend till smooth. Adjust the speed of your blender from low to high. You may garnish with chopped blueberries. Your brunch is ready. Enjoy!

Cool Mint and Cucumber Smoothie

Ingredients
1 cup chopped cucumber (peeled)
¼ cup finely chopped mint leaves
1/3 cup concentrated apple juice (unsweetened)
¼ cup chilled water
5-6 ice cubes

Preparation
Blend unsweetened apple juice, chopped cucumber and chopped mint leaves in an electronic blender. Blend till smooth. Now add chilled water and ice and blend again thoroughly. You may garnish with fresh mint leaves. You may have this smoothie as a healthy snack. Enjoy!

Mango Smoothie with Peach

Ingredients

2/3 cup mango cubes
2/3 cup peach nectar
2/3 cup peach slices
6 ounce of organic yoghurt (low fat)
1 tsp honey

Preparation

Add frozen peach slices, frozen mango cubes, organic yoghurt and peach nectar in a blending jar. Process the ingredients till they are pureed. Add honey and give a quick blend again. You may garnish with thin strawberry slices. You breakfast smoothie is ready. Enjoy!

Tofu Blackberry Smoothie with Walnuts

Ingredients

2 cups peach slices (frozen)
2 tsp f walnuts (finely chopped)
1 cup blackberries
2 tsp lemon juice
1 cup freshly squeezed orange juice
¼ cup honey
4 ounce silken tofu (chopped)

Preparation

Blend peach slices, blackberries, lemon juice, orange juice, silken tofu and honey in a blending jar. Blend till smooth. Top it with chopped walnuts. Your breakfast smoothie is ready. Enjoy!

Vanilla and Peanut Butter Smoothie

Ingredients

2 cups of vanilla yoghurt
1 tsp of flaxseed (crushed)
½ cup soy milk (vanilla)
1 tsp honey
½ cup milk (fat free)
1 tsp peanut butter
1/3 cup cubed silken tofu

Preparation

Blend all the ingredients except flaxseed in a blending jar. Garnish it with flaxseed while serving. Your breakfast smoothie is ready. Enjoy!

Pineapple Yoghurt Smoothie

Ingredients

2 cups vanilla yoghurt (low fat)
¼ cup coconut milk
1 cup pineapple juice
¼ tsp ginger (-peeled and chopped)
6 ice cubes

Preparation

Combine pineapple juice, vanilla yoghurt, coconut milk and ginger in a blending jar. Blend till smooth. Add ice cubes and blend till they are smoothly mixed. Garnish with thin pineapple slice. Serve as breakfast. Enjoy!

Kiwi Soy Milk Smoothie

Ingredients

4 kiwifruits peeled and cubed
1 tsp honey
2 bananas
1 ½ cup soy milk (low fat)
4 green tea bags (fruit flavoured)

Preparation

Refrigerate banana slices and cubed kiwifruits in a plastic bag for half an hour. Add green tea bags in boiling soy milk and keep it for 3 minutes. Remove the tea bags and strain soy milk and tea mixture. Add honey and let it cool. Now add green tea and soy milk mixture and all other fruits in a blending jar. Blend till smooth. Your breakfast smoothie is ready. Enjoy!

Mango Lime Smoothie

Ingredients

1 ½ cup mango (peeled and chopped)
¼ cup lime juice (freshly squeezed)
1 tsp brown sugar
1 ½ cups milk (fat free)
½ cup ice cubes
Thin lemon slices (for garnish)

Preparation

Combine chopped mango, freshly squeezed lime juice, low fat milk and brown sugar in an electronic jar. Blend till the ingredients are smoothly pureed. Your smoothie is ready. Top it with thin lemon slice and ice cubes and serve it. Enjoy!

Orange Cinnamon Smoothie

Ingredients

1 cup orange juice (freshly squeezed)
1 banana (ripe)
1 cup vanilla yoghurt (low fat)
A pinch salt
A pinch cinnamon (freshly powered)

Preparation

Peel and slice the banana. Combine banana slices, vanilla yoghurt and orange juice in a blending jar. Blend for 30 seconds. Add salt and powered cinnamon. Blend again till smooth. Your healthy and delicious evening snack is ready. Enjoy!

Energizing Blueberry Smoothie

Ingredients

1 cup blueberries (frozen)
6 ounces raspberry yoghurt (low fat)
2/3 cup milk (fat free)
4 ounce silken tofu
2 tsp raspberry syrup

Preparation

Combine frozen blueberries, low fat raspberry yoghurt, fat free milk, silken tofu and raspberry syrup in a blending jar. Blend till all the ingredients are pureed smoothly. Serve the smoothie as a snack. Enjoy!

Sweet Cherries Smoothie

Ingredients

2 cups sweet cherries
¼ cup honey
1 ½ cups ice cubes
1 ½ cups plain yoghurt (fat free)

Preparation

Add fat free yogurt, honey and sweet cherries in an electronic blending jar. Blend for around 30 seconds. Now add ice cubes and blend again till all the ingredients are smoothly pureed. Adjust the speed of your blender from low to high. Garnish the drink with sweet cherries. Your evening snack is ready. Enjoy!

Orange-Berries Smoothie

Ingredients

¼ cup orange juice
¼ cup mixed berries (frozen)
1 medium sized banana (sliced)
1/3 cup low fat dry milk

8 ounces vanilla yoghurt (fat free)
1 tsp sugar
4-5 pieces of ice cubes

Preparation

Combine mixed berries, low fat dry milk, orange juice and vanilla yoghurt and blend till the ingredients are smoothly mixed. Blend a few pieces of ice cubes if required. Serve with few slices of strawberry. This smoothie can be perfect for breakfast or lunch. Enjoy!

Mango Sunshine Smoothie

Ingredients

½ cup chopped mango (peeled)
4 small apricots (peeled and chopped)
6 ounce lemon yoghurt (low fat)
2/3 cup nectarine (chopped)

⅛ tsp lemon rind (grated)
1 cup cantaloupe (chopped)
¼ cup mango nectar
1 cup cubed ice

Preparation

Refrigerate chopped mango in a zip lock plastic bag for an hour. Combine all other ingredients except mango and ice in a blender. Blend well. Add frozen mango and ice and blend till smooth. Enjoy!

Oatmeal Smoothie with Strawberry

Ingredients

½ cup rolled oats
½ tsp vanilla extract
1 medium sized banana

2 tsp regular sugar
1 cup soy milk
13 strawberries (frozen)

Preparation

Peel and cut the banana into chunks. Combine soy milk, vanilla extract, white sugar, oats, and strawberries in a blending jar. Blend them till smooth. This smoothie is ideal for your breakfast. Enjoy!

Melon and Kiwi Smoothie

½ cup vanilla soy milk (low fat)
1 banana (frozen)
6 ounce of yogurt (fat free)
1 cup spinach leaves
1 cup honey melon (cubed)
1 kiwifruit (cubed)

Preparation

Peel and slice the frozen banana. Combine kiwifruit, vanilla soy milk, banana slices, yoghurt, melon and spinach leaves in a blender. Blend till all the ingredients are pureed smoothly. Serve it as a snack. Enjoy!

Lean Green Smoothie

Ingredients

1 cup spinach leaves
3 packets zero calorie sweetener
1 sliced kiwifruit
1 cup almond milk (unsweetened)
½ chopped pear
½ inch ginger (grated)
1 tsp chia seeds
1 cup cubed ice

Preparation

Combine spinach leaves, kiwifruit, pear, almond milk, chia seeds, ginger and 0 calorie sweetener in an electronic blending jar. Blend till the ingredients are smoothly mixed. Add ice cubes and blend again. Enjoy!

Mango Vanilla Smoothie

Ingredients

2 cups mango cubes (frozen)
1 carton vanilla yoghurt (fat free)
½ cup mango nectar
2 tsp honey
2 to 4 Mint Leaves

Preparation

Combine mango cubes, mango nectar and vanilla yoghurt in an electronic blending jar. Blend till smooth. Add honey and blend well till it gets mixed thoroughly. Adjust the speed of your blender from low to high. Garnish with fresh mint leaves. Your evening snack is ready. Enjoy!

Rehydrating Watermelon Smoothie

Ingredients

1 cup watermelon cubes (frozen)
4-5 fresh mint leaves
½ cup coconut water
2 tsp lime juice
½ cup cubed ice

Preparation

Take a blending jar and combine watermelon cubes, fresh mint leaves, coconut water and lime juice. Blend till smooth. Add ice cubes and blend again thoroughly. You may serve this smoothie with lunch. Enjoy!

Spiced Banana Smoothie

Ingredients

2 bananas (ripe)
½ tsp cinnamon (powered)
⅛ tsp nutmeg (powered)
2 cups vanilla kefir
½ cup cubed ice

Preparation

Peel and cut the banana into slices. Combine vanilla kefir, banana slices, powered cinnamon and powered nutmeg in an electronic blending jar. Blend till all the ingredients are smoothly pureed. Add ice and blend till the ice cubes are mixed properly. Your breakfast smoothie is ready. Enjoy!

Tangy Berry Smoothie

Ingredients

1 ¼ cup berries
½ tsp vanilla extract
¾ cups yoghurt (low fat)
½ cup orange juice
1 tsp wheat germ (toasted)
2 tsp dry milk (non-fat)
1 tsp honey

Preparation

Combine berries, vanilla extract, low fat yoghurt, orange juice, dry milk and toasted wheat germ in a blending jar. Blend till smooth. Add honey to it and blend thoroughly again. Enjoy!

Honeydew Mint Smoothie

Ingredients

2 cups honeydew
2 Bartlett pears (ripe)
½ cup white grape juice
½ cup apple juice
½ cup fresh mint leaves
½ cup ice cubes

Preparation

Combine honeydew, ripe Barlett pears, white grape juice, apple juice and fresh mint leaves in a blender. Blend till the ingredients are pureed well. Add ice cubes and blend again thoroughly. Adjust the speed of your blender from low to high. Your evening delicious and healthy snack is ready in just few minutes. Enjoy!

Peanut Butter and Banana Smoothie

Ingredients

1 frozen banana
½ cup low fat milk
1 tsp peanut butter
4-5 ice cubes

Preparation

Cut frozen banana into slices. Combine banana slices, low fat milk and peanut butter in an electronic blending jar. Blend till the ingredients are smoothly pureed. Add 4-5 ice cubes and blend again till smooth. Your breakfast smoothie is ready. Enjoy!

Cocoa and Banana Smoothie

Ingredients

½ cup silken tofu
2 tsp cocoa powder (unsweetened)
½ cup soy milk
1 ripe banana
1 tsp honey

Preparation

Peel and slice the banana. Refrigerate it for around 30 minutes. Combine frozen banana slices, honey, soy milk, tofu and cocoa powder in a blending jar. Blend till all the ingredients are smoothly pureed. You may serve this smoothie as lunch. Enjoy!

Cherry and Chocolate Smoothie

Ingredients

1 cup vanilla flavored almond milk (unsweetened)
2 tsp chocolate protein powder
2 cups cherries (frozen)
2 handfuls baby spinach leaves
½ cup water

Preparation

Blend unsweetened almond milk, chocolate protein powder, frozen cherries, baby spinach leaves and a cup of water in an electronic blending jar till all the ingredients are pureed well. Adjust the speed of your blender from low to high. Your breakfast smoothie is ready. Enjoy!

Mixed Berries and Cereal Smoothie

Ingredients

1 cup blueberries (frozen)
1 cup strawberries (frozen)
2 cup soy milk (vanilla)
1 tsp agave nectar
½ cup whole grain cereal.

Preparation

Take a blender jar and combine frozen blueberries, frozen strawberries, soy milk, and whole grain cereal and agave nectar. Blend till all the ingredients till they are pureed smoothly. Garnish the smoothie with strawberry slices. Serve the smoothie for breakfast. Enjoy!

Raspberry Vanilla Smoothie

Ingredients

¾ cup raspberries (fresh)
1 handful mixed greens
½ cup strawberries (frozen)
1 cup vanilla flavored almond milk

Preparation

Combine fresh raspberries, mixed greens and frozen strawberries in a blending jar. Blend for around 30 seconds. Now add in vanilla flavored almond milk and give a quick blend to it. Serve as breakfast. Enjoy!

Blueberry with Soy Milk Smoothie

Ingredients

1 cup vanilla flavored soy milk
½ cup blueberries
4 oz. honey flavored yoghurt
¼ cup graham crackers

Preparation

Take an electronic blending jar and combine vanilla flavored soy milk, fresh blueberries, honey flavored yoghurt in it. Blend for around 30 seconds. Now add in graham crackers to it. Blend again thoroughly till the ingredients are pureed. Your smoothie is now ready to be served. Enjoy!

Cocoa and Avocado Smoothie

Ingredients

3 tsp cocoa powder (unsweetened)
1 banana (ripe)
1 avocado (ripe)
2 tsp agave nectar
1 cup almond milk (vanilla)

Preparation

Peel banana and avocado. Deseed avocado. Take a blending jar and combine almond milk, agave nectar, ripe avocado, ripe banana and cocoa powder. Blend till smooth. Serve this as breakfast. Enjoy!

Salad Smoothie

Ingredients

3 tsp fresh lime juice
1 apple (with peel)
2 stalks celery
1 cucumber (cut in slices)
Handful mixed greens
1 frozen banana (cut into slices)
½ cup cold water
½ cup vanilla yoghurt (frozen)

Preparation

Combine fresh lime juice and water in a blender. Blend well. Now add apple, cucumber, celery, mixed greens, banana and yoghurt. Blend thoroughly again adjusting the speed of your blender from low to high. Serve as breakfast or snack. Enjoy!

Spinach and Banana Smoothie

Ingredients

1 banana (ripe)
Handful spinach leaves
1 cup berries (frozen)
½ cup chilled water

Preparation

Peel and cut the banana into slices. Combine spinach and water in a blending jar. Blend till the spinach gets smoothly pureed. Now add banana slices and frozen berries to it and blend again thoroughly. Your smoothie is ready to be served. Serve as breakfast or lunch.

Oatmeal and Apple Smoothie

Ingredients

½ apple (cored)
¾ cup chilled apple juice
2 tsp protein powder (vanilla)
½ cup baby carrots (frozen)
4 oz. vanilla yoghurt
½ cup oatmeal (uncooked)

Preparation

Combine apple juice and cored apple in a blending jar. Blend till smooth. Add all other ingredients and blend till they are pureed well. Your breakfast is smoothie.

Spicy Peach Smoothie

Ingredients

¼ cup soy milk
¾ cup fresh orange juice
1 tsp grated ginger
2 peaches (ripe)
½ tsp cinnamon
6-7 ice cubes

Preparation

Combine soy milk, grated ginger, fresh orange juice and ripe peaches in an electronic blending jar. Blend for around 30 seconds. Now add freshly powered cinnamon and ice. Blend thoroughly till smooth. Garnish with thin peach slices. Your evening snack is ready. Enjoy!

Grapes and Peanut Butter Smoothie

Ingredients

½ cup vanilla flavored soymilk
2 tsp vanilla flavored protein powder
1 cup red grapes
½ cup peanut butter
1 cup ice cubes

Preparation

Combine red grapes and soy milk in a blender. Blend till smooth. Now add protein

Carrot and Apple Smoothie

Ingredients

8 baby carrots (organic)
1 Brae burn apple
½ cup apple juice

Preparation

Peel the baby carrots and chop them into thin slices. Core and chop the apple. Take a blending jar and combine baby carrots, chopped apple and apple juice in it. Blend till the ingredients are smoothly pureed. Blend thoroughly again adjusting the speed of your blender from low to high. If you want you may add ice cubes and blend again. Serve as breakfast or snack. Enjoy!

Kale with Fruits Smoothie

Ingredients

1 large sized piece of raw Kale
1 cup apple juice
1 cup water
½ cup frozen peach (cut into slices)
½ cup frozen mango (cut into cubes)
½ banana (ripe)
1 cup strawberry yoghurt (frozen)

Preparation

Blend raw kale and apple juice in a blender till the kale is pureed smoothly. Now add the other ingredients and blend again thoroughly. Serve as breakfast. Enjoy!

Melon and Cucumber Smoothie

Ingredients

2 cups sweet melon
½ cup cucumber (unpeeled)
1 tsp fresh lime juice
6-7 mint leaves

8 ounces almond milk (unsweetened)
3 cups dandelion greens
1 frozen banana (sliced)

Preparation

Put banana, almond milk and lime juice in blending jar. Blend for 30 seconds. Now add melon, unpeeled cucumber, mint and dandelion greens and blend till smooth. You may have this smoothie with your breakfast. Enjoy!

Pear and Orange Smoothie

Ingredients

1 orange
1 pear

1 lettuce (organic)
Mixed berries (handful)

Preparation

Chop lettuce coarsely. Peel the orange and remove its seed. Combine chopped lettuce and very little water in your blender. Blend till smooth. Now add orange, pear and mixed berries to it. Blend till all the ingredients are smoothly pureed. You may also use frozen berries. Serve as breakfast. Enjoy!

Cereals and Cinnamon Smoothie

Ingredients

1 ½ cups almond milk
1 ¾ cups cereal

1 frozen banana
⅛ tsp powered cinnamon

Preparation

Cut the frozen banana into slices. Combine almond milk, banana slices and cereal in a blender. Blend till the ingredients are smoothly pureed. Top it with banana slices. Sprinkle powered cinnamon on it. Serve it as breakfast or lunch. Enjoy!

Strawberry Smoothie with Orange

Ingredients
½ cup strawberries (fresh)
1 cup orange sherbet
½ cup ice cubes

Preparation
Refrigerate orange sherbet for 30 to 45 minutes. This will help in blending it. Combine fresh strawberries and orange sherbet in an electronic blending jar. Blend till smooth. Now add ice cubes in it. Blend again thoroughly. Adjust the speed of your blender from low to high. Garnish with thin strawberry slices. Enjoy!

Vanilla Pumpkin Smoothie

Ingredients
1 can of frozen pumpkin
½ cup milk (low fat)
½ cup frozen yoghurt (vanilla flavored)
½ tsp cinnamon
¼ tsp nutmeg
½ tsp vanilla extract
¼ tsp powered cloves

Preparation
Combine frozen pumpkin, milk, yoghurt, cinnamon, nutmeg, vanilla extract and powered cloves in an electronic blending jar. Blend until smooth. Your smoothie is ready to be served. You may have the smoothie for lunch. Enjoy!

Grapefruit and Mixed Berries Smoothie

Ingredients
1 cup grapefruit juice
1 banana
3 tsp yoghurt
1 cup mixed berries (frozen)

Preparation
Combine all the ingredients in an electronic blending jar. Blend till all the ingredients are smoothly pureed. Your breakfast smoothie is ready in a few minutes. Enjoy!

Pineapple-Orange Smoothie

Ingredients

1 cup pineapple cubes (frozen)
½ cup orange juice (chilled)
1 cup mango cubes (frozen)
1 ½ cups water
1 tsp of chia seeds

Preparation

Combine pineapple cubes, mango cubes, chilled orange juice and water in a blender. Blend till they are smoothly pureed. Add a teaspoon of chia seeds and give a quick blend. Your smoothie is ready. Enjoy!

Green Morning Smoothie

Ingredients

1 cup orange juice
2 cups frozen peaches
1 cup baby spinach
15 oz. yoghurt
1 cup chilled water

Preparation

Take an electronic blending jar. Combine all the ingredients and blend till smooth. Your breakfast smoothie is ready to be served. Enjoy!

Orange Vanilla Smoothie

Ingredients

1 cup fresh orange juice
6 oz. vanilla flavored yoghurt
½ cup orange sherbet
½ cup chilled milk

Preparation

Combine orange juice, orange sherbet, vanilla yoghurt and chilled milk in a blending jar. Blend till the ingredients are pureed smoothly. You may now serve the smoothie. Enjoy!

Mango Smoothie with Mint

Ingredients

½ cup mint leaves
2 ounces spinach leaves
1 cup almond milk (unsweetened)
¼ cup lime juice
1 large mango (cubed)
6 cubes ice
Sugar- As per taste

Preparation

Add mint leaves, spinach leaves, almond milk, lime juice, chopped ripe mango and ice cubes in a blending jar. Blend it till smooth, if required add sugar and blend it again till the sugar gets mixed. This smoothie can be served in breakfast.Enjoy!

Healthy Kefir Smoothie

Ingredients

1 cup Kefir
1 peach
1 beet
½ cup mixed berries
1 carrot
½ avocado
A handful of spinach
1 banana (ripe)
1 apple

Preparation

Peel and deseed the apple. Chop beet and carrots. Scoop out the flesh of avocado. Combine kefir and spinach in a blender. Blend till smooth. Add all other ingredients and blend again. Enjoy!

Apple Smoothie with Peanut Butter

Ingredients

1 apple
2 tsp peanut butter
½ cup vanilla flavored yoghurt (frozen)
½ cup water

Preparation

Peel the apple. Deseed it. Combine apple, peanut butter, and frozen vanilla yoghurt in an electronic blending jar. Blend till smooth. Adjust the speed of your blender from low to high. Your smoothie is ready. Enjoy!

Creamy Chocolate Milk Smoothie

Ingredients

1 cup cold chocolate milk
2 tsp vitamin powder (chocolate flavored)
¼ cup peanut butter
½ avocado
¾ cup ice cubes

Preparation

Combine chocolate milk, avocado, peanut butter and vitamin powder in a blending jar. Blend till the ingredients are mixed smoothly. Now add the ice and blend again till smooth. The evening snack is ready. Enjoy!

Sweet Potato Smoothie with Peach

Ingredients

1 medium sized sweet potato
1 cup mango juice
1 cup peach (frozen)
½ banana (frozen)
½ cup water

Preparation

Boil the sweet potatoes and peel them. Refrigerate the cooked potatoes. Cut banana into slices. Combine sweet potatoes, banana slices, frozen peach and mango juice in a blender. Blend till all the ingredients are smoothly pureed. Adjust the speed of your blender from low to high. Your evening snack is ready to be served. Enjoy!

Plum Yoghurt Smoothie

Ingredients

3 plums
¼ cup yoghurt
1 ½ cup peaches
¼ cup water

Preparation

Deseed the plum. Slice the peaches. Do not peel off the plums as it gives a pinkish purple color to the smoothie. Take a blending jar and combine plum, yoghurt, peaches and water in it. Blend till smooth. Adjust the speed of your blender from low to high. Serve this as snack. Enjoy!

Pineapple Vanilla Smoothie

Ingredients

15 oz. pineapple juice
1 cup vanilla yoghurt
6-7 ice cubes

Preparation

Take a blending jar. Combine pineapple juice and vanilla yoghurt in a blender. Blend for around 30 seconds. Add 6 to 7 ice cubes and blend till smooth. Garnish with thin pineapple slices. Serve the smoothie as a breakfast or snack. Enjoy!

Milky Banana Smoothie

Ingredients

2 bananas (ripe)
1 cup vanilla flavored yoghurt (low fat)
2 tsp protein powder
1 tsp vanilla extract
1 cup chilled water

Preparation

Peel and slice the banana. Add chilled water, banana slice and vanilla yoghurt in an electronic blending jar. Blend till the ingredients are smoothly pureed. Add protein powder and vanilla extract and blend again thoroughly. Enjoy!

Creamy Banana Smoothie

Ingredients

½ cup vanilla yoghurt (fat free)
2 tsp of flaxseeds (powered)
½ cup milk (low fat)
1 tsp honey
1 tsp peanut butter
1 banana (ripe)
¼ tsp vanilla extract

Preparation

Blend all the ingredients in a blender till smooth. Serve as breakfast. Enjoy!

Honey Blackberries Smoothie

Ingredients

2 cups blackberries (frozen)
1 cup chilled apple juice
1 cup yoghurt
1 banana (ripe)
¼ cup honey

Preparation

Combine blackberries, yoghurt, apple juice, ripe banana and honey in a blending jar. Blend till the ingredients are smoothly pureed. Your breakfast smoothie is ready to be served. Enjoy!

Guava Smoothie with Strawberry

Ingredients

½ cup guava nectar
6 ounces strawberry yoghurt (fat free)
1 cup strawberry (cut into quarters)
1 frozen banana (ripe)
5-6 ice cubes

Preparation

Peel and cut the banana into thin slices. Place all the ingredients in an electronic blender and blend till the ingredients are smoothly pureed. Your evening smoothie is ready to be served. Enjoy!

Cucumber Tomato Smoothie

Ingredients

2 cups chilled tomato juice
½ cup finely chopped cucumber
2 tsp freshly squeezed lemon juice
¾ tsp Chile sauce
5-6 ice cubes
2 tsp Worcestershire sauce

Preparation

Combine chilled tomato juice, finely chopped cucumber, lemon juice, Worcester sauce and chilli sauce in an electronic blending jar. Blend till the ingredients are smoothly pureed. Add 5-6 ice cubes and blend till smooth. Your smoothie is ready to be served. Enjoy!

Grape and Raspberry Smoothie

Ingredients

1 cup raspberries (frozen)
½ cup chilled grape juice
6 ounce strawberry yoghurt (low fat)
2 tsp honey
½ tsp freshly squeezed lime juice

Preparation

Combine frozen raspberries, chilled grape juice, strawberry yoghurt and lime juice in an electronic blending jar. Blend for around 30 seconds. Now add honey to it and blend again till smooth. Your breakfast smoothie is ready. Enjoy!

Chocolate Cinnamon Smoothie

Ingredients

1 cup vanilla flavored soy milk
½ cup silken tofu
1 tsp cocoa (unsweetened)
1 cup dark chocolate sorbet
A pinch powered cinnamon
⅛ tsp vanilla extract
2 tsp honey

Preparation

Combine all the ingredients in an electronic blending jar. Blend till the ingredients are smoothly pureed. You may serve the smoothie as an evening snack. Enjoy!

Coconut and Lime Smoothie

Ingredients

½ cup chilled coconut milk
¼ tsp lime rind (grated)
1 tsp freshly squeezed lime juice
6 ounce lime yoghurt (fat free)
5-6 cubes ice
2 tsp honey

Preparation

Combine lime rind, lime juice, honey and coconut milk in a blending jar. Blend till smooth. Now add lime flavored yoghurt and ice cubes to it. Blend till the ingredients are mixed well. Serve as an evening snack. Enjoy!

Mixed Berries and Oats Smoothie

Ingredients

1 cup blackberries
1 tsp honey
½ cup strawberries (cut into slices)
¼ cup cooked oatmeal
¼ cup chilled milk
½ tsp honey
½ cup cubed ice

Preparation

Combine all the ingredients except ice cubes in an electronic blending jar. Blend till smooth. Now add in the ice cubes and blend again thoroughly. Serve as breakfast. Enjoy!

Refreshing Berry Orange Smoothie

Ingredients

1 cup blueberries (frozen)
2 oranges
1 cup raspberries (frozen)
4-5 ice cubes (optional)

Preparation

Peel the chop the oranges into small chunks. Put blueberries, oranges, raspberries in a blending jar. Blend them till they are smooth and frothy. You must adjust the speed of the blender from low to high. Add some ice cubes and blend it again. Although, ice cubes are optional. Your smoothie is ready. This is a perfect smoothie for your breakfast. Enjoy!

Pineapple with Almond Milk Smoothie

Ingredients

1 cup homemade almond milk (unsweetened)
1 cup packed kale
½ cup pineapple juice
1 banana
½ cup pineapple cubes

Preparation

Chop the packed kale into small cubes. Peel the banana and cut into thin slices. Put all the ingredients except the unsweetened almond milk in a blending jar. Blend them till they are pureed well. Now add almond milk and blend again. This smoothie is best suited in breakfast. Enjoy!

Green Tea and Melon Smoothie

Ingredients

½ honeydew melon
¼ cup almond milk
1 banana (frozen)
2 bags green tea
1 tsp honey

Preparation

Take ¾ cup of boiling water. Add the tea bags in the boiling water. Keep it for ten minutes. Cut the honeydew melon into small chunks. Peel the banana. Put all the ingredients of the smoothie in a blending jar and blend till smooth. You may have this smoothie for lunch. Enjoy!

Pineapple Smoothie with Coconut

Ingredients

1 cup chopped pineapple
¼ cup vanilla yoghurt
1 tsp coconut flakes (sweetened)
¼ cup coconut milk
½ cup ice

Preparation

Put chopped pineapple, vanilla yoghurt, coconut flakes and coconut milk in a blending jar. Blend them till smooth. Now add the ice and blend again. Garnish the smoothie with sweetened coconut flakes. You may have this filling smoothie as lunch or a snack.

Green Tea and Blueberry Smoothie

Ingredients

½ cup blueberries (frozen)
1 tsp agave nectar
2 cups green tea

Preparation

Green tea must be cooled to the room temperature. Add blueberries in an ice cube tray. Refrigerate it. After it is done, add frozen blueberries and green tea in a blending jar. Pour the agave nectar in remaining green tea. Blend thoroughly till smooth. Enjoy!

Mango Coconut Smoothie

Ingredients

2 sweet mangoes
2 cups coconut water
Small pinch cayenne powder
3 tsp lime juice
½ tsp cayenne pepper

Preparation

Peel the mangoes. Chop them. Add mango chunks, coconut water and lime juice in a blending jar. Blend for 30 seconds till all the ingredients are mixed well. Add a pinch of cayenne powder and blend again. You can try this smoothie as a snack or lunch. Enjoy!

Chocolate and Cherry Smoothie

Ingredients

¼ cup sweet cherries (frozen)
¼ cup low fat milk
1 tsp cocoa powder (unsweetened)
¼ cup vanilla yoghurt (without sugar)
1 tsp honey
5 cubes ice

Preparation

Take a blending jar and add sweet cherries, milk, vanilla yoghurt and unsweetened cocoa powder. Blend the ingredients till smooth. Now add ice cubes and blend again. Put a teaspoon of honey and stir with a spoon. This is a lovely breakfast smoothie for everyone who loves chocolate. Enjoy!

Blueberry Smoothie with Almond Butter

Ingredients

1 ½ cup blueberries (frozen)
1 tsp lime juice
2 tsp flax seed
3-4 dates
1 banana (ripe)
2 cups chilled water

Preparation

Peel and cut the banana into thin slices. The dates must be pitted. Add banana, blueberries, flax seeds, dates and lime juice in a blending jar. Blend for 30 seconds. Add water and blend till all the ingredients turn smooth and frothy. Adjust the speed of your blender from low to high. You may have this smoothie in your breakfast or evening snack. Enjoy!

Go Green Smoothie

Ingredients

5 kale leaves
½ cup parsley sprigs
½ cup pineapple
½ cup mango
7 romaine leaves
1 inch f ginger

Preparation

Chop romaine leaves and kale leaves. Cut mango and pineapple into small pieces. The ginger must be chopped finely. Add all the ingredients in a blending jar. Puree them till smooth. You can have this smoothie for breakfast. Enjoy!

Chilled Pomegranate and Berry Smoothie

Ingredients

1 cup pomegranate juice (unsweetened)
2 cups mixed berries (frozen)
1 cup chilled water
4-5 ice cubes (optional)

Preparation

Combine pomegranate juice, mixed berries and a cup of water in a blending jar. Puree all the ingredients till they are smooth. You may add 4-5 cubes of ice and blend well. You can have this delicious smoothie for breakfast. Enjoy!

Blueberry and Kiwi Smoothie

Ingredients

2 ripe bananas (frozen)
8 ounces fat free yoghurt
¼ tsp almond extract
4 tsp honey
1 cup blueberries (frozen)
3 kiwifruits
1 cup ice cubes

Preparation

Peel and cut bananas and kiwifruits. Add banana, fat free yoghurt, almond extract, honey, blueberries and kiwifruits in a blending jar. Blend till the ingredients turn smooth. Add a cup of ice cubes and blend again into a smooth mixture. You can have this smoothie for breakfast. Enjoy!

Banana and Greens Smoothie

Ingredients

1 cup collard greens
1 apple
½ cup parsley leaves
1 banana (ripe)
3 cups water

Preparation

Remove the stems of the collard greens. Chop apple, parsley leaves and collard greens. Peel the banana and cut into thin slices. Add parsley leaves, collard greens, apple, banana and water in a blending jar. Blend till all the ingredients are pureed well. You may try this smoothie in your breakfast. Enjoy!

Tofu Smoothie with Fruits

Ingredients

1 cup mixed berries (frozen)
½ cup white grape juice
1 banana (ripe)
3 ounce silken tofu
1 tsp honey

Preparation

Peel the cut the banana into small sized pieces. Combine frozen mixed berries, grape juice, pieces of banana and silken tofu in a blending jar. Puree all the ingredients till smooth. Add a teaspoon of honey and blend again. Enjoy!

Cinnamon and Berries Smoothie

Ingredients

1 ½ cup blackberries (frozen)
½ cup yoghurt (low fat)
½ cup buttermilk (low fat)
⅛ tsp cinnamon (powered)
2 tsp honey

Preparation

Combine frozen blackberries, low fat yoghurt and low fat buttermilk in a blending jar. Blend for around 30 seconds. Add honey and powered cinnamon powder and blend again thoroughly till all the ingredients are smoothly puréed. Begin your day with this healthy low fat refreshing smoothie. . Enjoy!

Oats and Ginger Berry Smoothie

Ingredients

½ cup water
½ cup blueberries (frozen)
½ cup plain yoghurt
2 tsp brown sugar

¼ cup rolled oats
½ cup ice
½ tsp ginger, grated

Preparation

Pour half cup of water in a blending jar. Add oats to water and allow it to soak for ten minutes. Now add brown sugar, grated ginger, frozen blueberries and ice in the blending jar. Blend till the ingredients are smooth. Try this smoothie for breakfast. Enjoy!

Creamy Cashew Smoothie

Ingredients

1 cup cashew nuts
1 tsp vanilla extract
1 cup boiling water

1 tsp agave nectar
1 cup ice cubes

Preparation

Add boiling water to the cashew nuts. Let the cashews rest in the water for around 15-20 minutes till the nuts soak water and become tender. Blend the cashew nuts with water for 3 to 4 minutes. Combine vanilla extract and ice and blend well. Add agave nectar as per taste. This smoothie is perfect as an evening snack. Enjoy!

Blueberry Smoothie with Flax Seeds

Frozen blueberries are just delicious in taste. The smoothie is quiet filling as it has banana in it. As it uses low-fat yoghurt and honey as sweetener, you do not have worrying about the calorie count.

Ingredients

1 cup plain yoghurt (low-fat)
1 banana (ripe)
1 cup blueberries (frozen)

4 tsp flax seeds
1 tsp honey

Preparation

Peel the banana. Cut it into small pieces. Combine banana, flax seeds, frozen blueberries and plain yoghurt in a blending jar. Blend till all the ingredients are pureed thoroughly. Add honey and blend again. Try this delicious and filling smoothing as an evening snack. Enjoy!

Mango and Yoghurt Smoothie

Ingredients
1 cup Greek vanilla yoghurt (low fat)
1 cup mango chunks
3 tsp concentrated orange juice (frozen)
1 cup chilled coconut water (without sugar)
2 cups ice cubes

Preparation
Add low fat yoghurt mango chunks, frozen orange juice and coconut water in a blending jar. Puree the ingredients till they are smooth. Add ice cubes and blend again. The smoothie is perfect after your morning workout session due to its hydrating nature. Enjoy!

Chamomile Banana Smoothie

Ingredients
1 cup chamomile tea
1 cup plain yoghurt (non-fat)
2 tsp maple syrup
1 banana

Preparation
Prepare chamomile tea let it cool at room temperature. Pour the tea in an ice cube tray and refrigerate. Peel and cut the banana into slices. Take a blending jar and add all the ingredients along with the tea cubes. Blend till the ingredients turn smooth. You can have this rich and creamy smoothie for breakfast. Enjoy!

Banana and Coffee Smoothie

Ingredients
1 banana (ripe)
½ cup black coffee (cold)
1 cup milk
2 tsp sugar
1 pinch cocoa powder
½ cup ice cubes

Preparation
Peel and cut the banana into thin slices. Now take a blending jar and combine milk, black coffee, sugar and banana. Blend for 30 seconds. Add ice and blend again till smooth and frothy. Garnish with a pinch of cocoa powder. You can have this smoothie for breakfast. Enjoy!

Strawberry Yoghurt Smoothie

Ingredients

1 ½ cup strawberries (frozen)
2 tsp of honey

1 banana (ripe)
¾ cup plain yoghurt (low fat)

Preparation

Peel and cut the banana into thick slices. Add low fat yoghurt, frozen strawberries and banana in a blending jar. Blend for 30 seconds. Pour 2 tsp of honey and blend well till smooth. Your delicious smoothie is ready. You can have it for breakfast or have on the go. Enjoy!

Healthy Green Smoothie

Ingredients

1 cup cucumber chunks
½ avocado
1 cup baby spinach
1 cup kiwifruit

1 cup vanilla yoghurt
¼ cup mint leaves
½ cup orange juice

Preparation

The avocado must be halved, peeled and pitted. Combine orange juice, cucumber, baby spinach, kiwifruit, mint leaves and avocado in a blending jar. Blend for around 30 seconds. Add vanilla yoghurt and blend till smooth. You can have this smoothie for breakfast. Enjoy!

Ginger Orange Smoothie

This is a perfect combination to feel refreshed on those lazy mornings; orange and ginger make a perfect blend of zesty flavors.

Ingredients

1 cup orange juice
1 banana (ripe)
2 tsp grated ginger

2 tsp honey
1 cup ice cubes

Preparation

Peel the banana and cut into thick slices. Add orange juice, banana slices, ginger and honey in a blending jar. Blend for about 30 seconds. Now add a cup of ice and blend again till smooth. Enjoy!

Buttermilk and Dates Smoothie

Ingredients

2 bananas (ripe)
11 dry dates
1 cup low fat buttermilk
1 cup ice cubes
2 tsp honey
1 pinch salt

Preparation

Peel the cut the banana into thick slices. Deseed the dry dates. Take a blender and combine banana slices, dates and butter milk. Blend for around 30 seconds. Add ice, salt and honey. Blend again till smooth. Your breakfast smoothie is ready in just a few minutes. Enjoy!

Mixed Berries Smoothie

Ingredients

1 banana (ripe)
6 ounce of vanilla yoghurt (low fat)
1 cup raspberries
½ cup blackberries
4 cubes of ice
2 tsp of honey

Preparation

Peel the banana and cut into pieces. Add raspberries, blackberries, vanilla yoghurt and banana in a blending jar. Blend till smooth. Add the ice cubes and honey and blend again till all the ingredients are mixed well. You may have this delicious smoothie as breakfast or as an appetizer in brunch. Enjoy!

Soy Milk and Strawberry Smoothie

Ingredients

1 cup soy milk
8 ounces of strawberries (frozen)
1 banana (ripe)
2 tsp of honey

Preparation

Peel the bananas and cut them. Add frozen strawberries, ripe banana and soy milk in a blending jar. Blend them till smooth. Now add honey and give a blend again. Adjust the speed of your blender from low to high. This will make your smoothie creamy and frothy. You may have this delicious smoothie for breakfast. Enjoy!

Antioxidant Pomegranate Smoothie

Ingredients

1 banana
1 cup pomegranate juice
¾ cup soy milk
2 tsp almonds
3 tsp protein powder (optional)
1 tsp honey
2-3 ice cubes

Preparation

Peel and cut the banana into thick pieces. Combine banana pieces, protein powder, pomegranate juice, almonds and soy milk in a blending jar. Blend them for around 30 seconds. Now add honey and ice cubes to it. Blend again till smooth. Your protein rich breakfast smoothie is ready. Enjoy!

Carrot and Red Beet Smoothie

Carrot and red beet smoothie is bright red in color and thick in texture. Ginger and lemon juice enhances the taste.

Ingredients

½ cup red beet
1 apple
1 pear (ripe)
2 tsp grated ginger
2 tsp lime juice
2 cups water
½ cup carrot.

Preparation

Peel the red beet and carrots and chop them. Cut the apple into small pieces. Add carrots and beets to boiling water. Let it boil for around ten minutes till they are tender. Allow them to cool. Now add grated ginger, lime juice, boiled beets and carrots, apple and pear in a blending jar. Blend all the ingredients thoroughly. You may have this smoothie for lunch. Enjoy!

Wheat Germ and Blackberry Smoothie

Ingredients

1 ½ cup blackberries (frozen)
2 tsp wheat germ (toasted)
1 banana (ripe)
1 cup orange juice

Preparation

Peel and cut the banana into thick pieces. Combine banana pieces, frozen blackberries, toasted wheat germ and a cup of orange juice in a blending jar. Blend till all the ingredients are pureed well. You may serve this healthy smoothie for breakfast. Enjoy!

Apple Ginger and Carrot Smoothie

Ingredients

1 cup carrot juice
1 medium sized green apple
1 cup orange juice
2 tsp honey
2 tsp grated ginger

Preparation

Pour carrot juice in an ice tray and freeze. Peel and chop the green apple. Add iced carrot juice, chopped green apple, orange juice and grated ginger in a blending jar. Blend till all the ingredients are pureed well. Add honey and blend again. Your breakfast smoothie is ready. Enjoy!

Cucumber and Melon Smoothie

Ingredients

2 cucumbers
2 cups honeydew melon (chopped)
1 cup pear juice
¼ cup mint leaves
2 tsp lime juice

Preparation

Peel and chop the cucumber. Add chopped cucumber, pear juice, fresh mint leaves, chopped honeydew melon and lime juice in a blending jar. Blend them till smooth. Adjust the speed of your blender from low to high. Serve the smoothie for breakfast. Enjoy!

Banana Smoothie with Peanut Butter

Ingredients

1 cup low fat milk
2 tsp honey
1 banana (ripe)
¼ cup peanut butter
½ cup ice cubes

Preparation

Peel the banana and cut it into slices. Combine banana slices, peanut butter and low fat milk in a blending jar. Blend for 30 seconds. Add honey and ice and blend thoroughly till all the ingredients are pureed. You may have this smoothie for breakfast or brunch. Enjoy!

Mango and Carrot Smoothie with Herbs

Ingredients

2 cups mango chunks (frozen)
1 cup fresh orange juice
¼ cup fresh mint or basil or tarragon
1 cup carrot juice

Preparation

Place chunks of mango, fresh carrot juice and fresh orange juice in a blending jar. Blend well for 30 seconds. Add mint leaves and blend thoroughly. Serve this smoothie in breakfast. Enjoy!

Pure Vegan Smoothie

Ingredients

1 sliced cucumber
3 cups fresh spinach leaves
1 cup green tea
1 tsp Lemon juice
1 Unadulterated ginger root
2-3 cups Honeydew melon

Preparation

Just add all the ingredients mentioned above into a blender and let it mix well by gradually increasing the speed. Half a minute of blending is enough for. Start your day with pure vegan smoothie. Enjoy!

Slushy Orange Smoothie

Ingredients

3 ounce frozen orange juice canned or concentrated
½ cup milk
½ cup or 40 ml water
½ tsp vanilla extract
¼ cup white sugar
5 ice cubes

Preparation

Mix the concentrated orange juice, water, milk, sugar and vanilla extract into a blender. Add ice cubes to the mixture. Let the mixture blend till it turns smooth. Your slushy orange smoothie is ready, pour it into glasses and serve cold. Enjoy!

Clean Breeze Smoothie

Ingredients

1 cucumber, chopped
2 ripe kiwis, peeled
1 cup ginger-flavored kombucha
½ cupplain Greek yogurt, low fat
6 ice cubes
2 tsp fresh cilantro leaves

Preparation

Combine all the above mentioned ingredients into a blender and let it blend until the mixture turns smooth. Can be had at any time of the day and is best served cold. Enjoy!

Creamsicle Breakfast Smoothie

Ingredients

1 cup fresh coconut water, cup1 cup mango chunks, fresh or frozen
1 cup vanilla Greek yogurt, low fat
3 tsp orange juice concentrate chilled
2 cups ice cubes

Preparation

Blend all the above mentioned ingredients in a blender including the ice and let it blend until it turns smooth and frothy. This refreshing smoothie is a great hydrator after work-outs. Enjoy!

Citrus Berry Smoothie

Ingredients

1 ¼ cup Fresh berries
¾ cup Plain yogurt, low-fat
½ cup Orange juice
2 tsp Dry milk, low fat
1 tsp wheat germ, roasted
1 tsp Honey
½ tsp Vanilla extract

Preparation

Add all the above mentioned ingredients into a blender and blend it gradually increasing the speed until the mixture turns creamy and smooth. This refreshing, nutritious smoothie can be had at any time of the day. Enjoy!

Coffee-Banana Tofu Shake

Ingredients

1 ¼ cup Low-fat milk
2 cups drained silken tofu
1 ripe banana
1-2 tsp Sugar
1 cup ice cubes
2 tsp instant coffee powder
(preferably espresso)
A pinch of cinnamon powder (optional)

Preparation

Combine all the ingredients mentioned above except cinnamon powder in a blender and let it blend until the mixture turns extremely frothy. Add more sugar if needed and pour it into a glass and you can now add cinnamon if you like. It is a great breakfast smoothie. Enjoy!

Spiced Banana Smoothie

Ingredients

2 ripe bananas
2 cups vanilla kefir
⅛ teaspoon powered nutmeg
½ teaspoon powered cinnamon
12 ice cubes
⅛ teaspoon powered allspice

Preparation

Just add all the above mentioned ingredients including ice cubes into a blender and blend in high speed until the mixture becomes smooth. Your healthy and delicious banana spice smoothie is ready which can be had any time of the day and is extremely good for health. Enjoy!

Strawberry Smoothie

Ingredients

1 cup fresh strawberries
1 tsp sugar (optional)
1 ice cubes (optional)
1 cup buttermilk
½ cup juice concentrate of chilled cranberry

Preparation

Combine all the ingredients mentioned above except sugar in a blender and blend it until it turns frothy and smooth. Add sugar to sweeten it more if you want. Can be had anytime of the day and is healthy and delicious at the same time. Enjoy!

Apricot Smoothie

Ingredients

1 ½ cup Light syrup of canned apricot halves
6 ice cubes
1 cup fresh yogurt
tsp sugar

Preparation

Place the canned apricot halves, yogurt and sugar into a blender, and the ice cubes as well. Let the mixture blend for some time until it becomes smooth and frothy. Your apricot smoothie is ready and is best served cold. A refreshing smoothie to start your day with and has great nutritional content. Enjoy!

Green Tea Smoothie

Ingredients

2 cups Chilled white grapes
1 medium sized ripe avocado
1 cup baby spinach
½ cup brewed green tea (cooled)
2 tsp honey

Preparation

Mix white grapes, avocado, fresh spinach and cooled green tea in a blender. Add honey for sweetening and let the mixture blend until it turns frothy and smooth. A refreshing drink to start your day with and green tea has various nutritious advantages. Enjoy!

Tropical Fruit Smoothie

Ingredients

1 banana, sliced
½ cup silken tofu or plain low fat yogurt
1/3 cups concentrated chilled passion fruit
½ cup water
1 cup canned pineapple
½ cup ice cubes
1 tsp wheat or oat bran (optional)

Preparation

Combine all the ingredients into a blender and blend until smooth and creamy. This drink is best had in the morning along with breakfast. Enjoy!

Banana-Berry Smoothie

Ingredients

1 ¼ cup orange juice
1 banana, medium sized peeled and sliced
½ cup silken tofu 1 cup chilled blueberries or blackberries or raspberries
1 cup ice cubes 1 tsp sugar (optional)

Preparation

Mix all the above mentioned ingredients into a blender and cover and blend until the mixture turns frothy and smooth. Add sugar to it if you want to sweeten it a little more. Yours refreshing breakfast smoothie is ready. Enjoy!

Melon-Ginger Smoothie

Ingredients

1 cup honeydew melon, chopped
1/3 cup kiwi chopped and peeled
½ ripe banana sliced
¼ cup white grape juice
½ tsp ginger juice
2 tsp lime juice
1/3 cup lemon sorbet
Ice ½ cup

Preparation

Combine all the ingredients mentioned above into a blender and blend until the mixture becomes smooth and creamy. This smoothie helps you revitalize after a hectic day. Enjoy!

Apricot Smoothie

Ingredients

2 cups canned apricots
6 ice cubes
1 cup plain yogurt low fat
tsp sugar (optional)

Preparation

Blend apricot along with syrup, ice cubes, and yogurt in a mixer until frothy. Serve it cool after refrigerating for a while for excellent taste. This can be served ideally in the breakfast. Enjoy!

Pomegranate Berries Smoothie

Ingredients

2 cups frozen combined berries
1 cup pomegranate extracts juice
1 medium banana
½ cup cottage cheese low
½ cup water

Preparation

Combine the fruits, pomegranate extract juice, bananas, cottage cheese and water in a blender; combine them until it is smooth. Serve. Enjoy!

Raspberry-Avocado Smoothie

Ingredients

1 cup grapes, peeled and pitted
¾ cup lemon juice
¾ cup the strawberry juice
½ cup frozen raspberries (not thawed)

Preparation

Add all the ingredients in a blender and puree. Serve cold

Citrus Berries Smoothie

Ingredients

1 ¼ cups berries
¾ cup simply yogurt low-fat
½ cup lemon juice
1 tsp. dry milk low fat
1 tsp. rice germ roasted
1 tsp. honey
½ tsp. vanilla extract

Preparation:

Add fresh fruits, lemon juice, dry milk, honey and vanilla extract in a blender and combine until it becomes smooth. Serve fresh. Enjoy!

Thermos-Ready Smoothie

Ingredients

1 cup combined berries frozen
½ banana
½ cup apple juice
¼ cup silken tofu

Preparation

Combine all ingredients in a blender; until it becomes smooth. Serve fresh. Enjoy!

Tropical Tofu Smoothie

Ingredients

2 cups mango chopped, frozen
½ cups blueberry juice
1 cup apple juice
¾ cup silken tofu
¼ cup the Orange juice
1 tsp. fresh grated orange zest

Preparation

Combine the Apple juice, blueberry juice, silken tofu, energy in a blender and combine until smooth. Enjoy!

Tropical Fruit Smoothie

Ingredients

1 cup sliced canned pineapple
1 apple, sliced
½ cup silken tofu or low fat yogurt
1/3 cup fruit concentrate, chilled
½ cup water
1 cup ice cubes
1 tsp rice wheat bran or oat rice bran (optional)

Preparation

Add the tofu (or yogurt), fruit extract, water ice cubes and rice wheat bran (or oat bran) to a blender. Churn to a smooth concoction. Serve cold. Enjoy!

Wake-Up Smoothie

Ingredients

1 ¼ cups lemon juice,
1 banana
1 banana
1 ¼ cups raspberries and blackberries,

½ cup silken tofu or yogurt low tofu
1 tsp. glucose or Splenda Granular (optional)

Preparation

Combine the lemon juice, apples, raspberries, blackberries, banana, tofu (or yogurt) and glucose in a blender. Blend until a creamy mixture is formed.Serve cold. Enjoy!

Banana-Berry Smoothie

Ingredients

1 to ¼ cup lemon juice
1 apples, peeled and sliced
1 cup: blueberries, blackberries, or raspberries

½ cup silken tofu
5 ice cubes
1 tsp glucose (optional)

Preparation

Combine the fresh lemon juice, apples, assorted berries, tofu and the ice cubes in a blender, combine creamy. Enjoy!

Banana-Cocoa Soy Smoothie

Rich in The smoothie is filling and refreshing.

Ingredients

1 banana
½ cup silken tofu
½ cup soya milk

tsp. unsweetened chocolate powder
1 tsp. honey

Preparation

Blend banana, tofu, soya milk, chocolate and honey in a mixer until it becomes smooth. Enjoy!

Banana Liven Smoothie

Ingredients
2 clean bananas
2 cups vanilla flavor kefir
½ tsp. cinnamon powder
⅛ tsp. nutmeg powder
⅛ tsp. allspice powder
12 ice cubes

Preparation
Combine the kefir, bananas, nutmeg, allspice and the ice in a blender; combine until it becomes smooth. Enjoy!

Coffee-Banana Tofu Smoothie

Ingredients
1 ¼ cups low-fat milk
½ cup silken tofu, (if using a shelf-stable box, choose soft), drained
1 banana
1-2 tsp sugar
2 tsp instant coffee powdered, ideally espresso
2 ice cubes
¼ tsp Powered nutmeg, (optional)

Preparation
Combine milk, tofu, banana, coffee, sugar, and ice cubes in a mixer. Blend until creamy, if needed. Enjoy!

Cantaloupe Smoothie

Ingredients
1 banana
¼ cantaloupe fine chopped
½ cup yogurt low fat
2 tsp. dry milk low fat
1 ½ tsp. lemon juice
2 tsp honey
½ tsp. vanilla extract

Preparation
Blend all ingredients in a blend until smooth and creamy. Serve cold. Enjoy Enjoy!

Clean Wind Smoothie

Ingredients

1 small cucumber, chopped
2 kiwis, peeled and chopped
1 cup kombucha ginger-flavored
½ cup yogurt (low fat)
2 tsp. cilantro leaves
6 ice cubes

Preparation

Combine cucumber, kiwis, kombucha, yogurt, cilantro and ice in blender; blend until smooth. Serve chilled. Enjoy!

Creamsicle Smoothie

Ingredients

1 cup authentic grape juice, chilled, without sugar
1 cup yogurt low fat, vanilla flavour
1 cup apple chopped
1 tsp. lemon juice concentrate
2 cups ice

Preparation

Blend grape juice, yogurt, the apples, lemon juice concentrate and ice in a mixer until smooth. Serve fresh. Enjoy!

Fresh Fruit Vanilla Smoothie.

Ingredients

1 cup yogurt low fat,
½ tsp vanilla essence
¼ cup fresh fruit juice, as per choice
1 ½ cups (assorted fresh fruits, or such as blueberries, raspberries, bananas or peaches

Preparation

Combine yogurt fruit juice and assorted fruits in a mixer until smooth. Enjoy!

Orange and Flax Seed Smoothie

Ingredients

2 cups of apple slices
1 cup carrot juice
2 cups orange juice
1 cup lemon juice
2 tsp. Powered flax seed
1 tsp. chopped clean ginger

½ tsp nutmeg powder

Preparation
Combine the apple, carrot, fruit juice, lemon juice, flax seed and nutmeg in blender; combination until smooth. Enjoy!

Good Natural Tea Smoothie

Ingredients
- 2 cups white- grapes, frozen
- 2 loaded cups baby spinach leaves
- 1 ½ cups brewed teas cooled
- 1 medium fresh avocado
- 2 tsp honey

Preparation:
Combine the, green spinach, teas, grape in a blender; combine until it is smooth. Enjoy!

Hawaiian Smoothie

Ingredients
- 1 cup fresh pineapple sliced
- ½ cup papaya peeled and sliced
- ¼ cup guava nectar
- 1 cup orange juice
- 1 tsp. grenadine
- ½ cup ice cubes

Preparation:
Blend all ingredients together until smooth. Enjoy!

Mango Lassi Smoothie

Ingredients
- 1 cup mango peeled and sliced
- 1/3 cup peach sorbet
- ½ cup vanilla yogurt low fat
- ¼ cup lemon juice

Preparation:
Blend all ingredients in a blender and serve. (The same recipe can be made by using buttermilk instead of the yogurt) Enjoy!

Melon-Ginger Smoothie

Ingredients

1 cup honeydew melon sliced
1/3 cup kiwi peeled sliced
½ banana, sliced
¼ cup white- grape juice

½ tsp. cinnamon powder
1/3 cup lemon sorbet
½ cup ice cubes

Preparation

Blend all ingredients in a mixer grinder. Serve cold Enjoy!

Pineapple-Coconut Frappe

Ingredients

1 ½ glasses pineapple sliced
1 cup milk low fat

1/3 cup grape juice
10 ice cubes

Preparation

Blend all ingredients in a blender until smooth. Enjoy!

Cherry Vanilla Smoothie

Ingredients

1 cup Unsweetened, frozen cherries
½ cup low fat milk
½ cup Low fat vanilla yogurt

½ tsp vanilla essence
4-5 ice cubes

Preparation

Take all the ingredients to a blender and blend them gradually increase the speed and make a smooth blend. This smoothie is rich in vitamins and minerals. Enjoy!

Avocado Blueberry Smoothie

Ingredients

1 cup crushed ice
1 can peach nectar
½ tsp powered cinnamon
1 tsp vanilla essence

1 ripe avocado
½ cup Blueberries

Preparation

Take a blender and add all the ingredients Blend at a high speed for about five minutes, until a creamy and smooth texture is formedEnjoy!

Strawberry Oatmeal Breakfast Smoothie

Ingredients

1 cup soy milk
½ cup rolled oats
1 banana, cut into pieces
14 strawberries frozen
½ tsp vanilla essence
1 tsp White sugar

Preparation

Blend all ingredients together until smooth. Serve as breakfastEnjoy!

All-Round Good Smoothie

Ingredients

½ cup milk low fat
1 cup Plain yogurt
2 Bananas chopped
¼ cup powdered protein supplement
1 ½ tsp flax seeds
2 tsp Honey
12-14 strawberries, frozen

Preparation

All the ingredients are to be taken in to a blender and are to be blended until they smooth.Enjoy!

Triple Berry Blend

Ingredients

½ cup Strawberries
½ cup Blueberries
½ cup Blackberries
2 cups Low-fat milk
5 Ice cubes
1 tsp Sugar (optional)

Preparation

Blend all the ingredients together in a blender until smooth. Enjoy!

Pineapple and Banana Smoothie

Ingredients

1 cup Pineapple juice
1 Banana, peeled and cut into pieces
1 cup Strawberries
1 tsp Vanilla essence
1 cup Vanilla yogurt

Preparation

Take all the ingredients to the blender, you can also add honey if you want added sweetness and blend them slowly until they attain a smooth texture. When the ingredients are properly combined and get the smooth texture, then the delicious and healthy smoothie is ready to be served.Enjoy!

Apricot-Almond Smoothie

Ingredients

2 cups apricot nectar
½ cup vanilla yogurt
2-3 tsp almond butter
½ cup ice cubes

Preparation

In a blender and pour all the ingredients to it and blend them slowly until a creamy texture is formed. When you get your desired consistency then the delicious smoothie is ready to be served. This drink can also be used to welcome your guests, as this smoothie can be a great replacement for any other meal and is liked by all. Enjoy!

Walnut toffee and Chocolate Smoothie

Ingredients

½ cup red grapes
¼ cup plain yogurt,
½ cup ice cubes
1 cup milk low fat
½ cup walnuts, 1 cup cantaloupe sliced
Toffee bits (optional)
2 tsp Chocolate powder

Preparation

Take all the ingredients in a blender and blend them gradually; increase the speed to get a good blend. When the desired creamy texture is prepared, then the delicious smoothie is ready to get served as your dessert. Enjoy!

Banana Caramel Smoothie

Ingredients

1 cup Low-fat vanilla yogurt
1 large banana
1 cup almond milk or soy milk

For garnishing, fat free caramel
A pinch of clove, cinnamon and ginger powder

Preparation

Add all the ingredients in the blender, except the caramel and blend them slowly until a creamy and smooth texture is formed. Season with spices as per taste. Now pour a part of caramel to the blender and give a final blend. When blended properly, serve the smoothie. Garnish with the remaining caramel. Enjoy!

Green Envy Avocado Smoothie

Ingredients

2 medium sized bananas
2 cups orange juice
1 cup strawberries
1 cup strawberry sherbet
1 cup ice cubes
2 Avocados

Preparation

The avocados used should be peeled and pitted and the bananas should be peeled and cut into pieces. Add all the ingredients to a blender and blend them till the desired consistency is formed. When you get a creamy texture, the delicious and healthy smoothie is ready to be served. Enjoy!

Peppermint Smoothie

Ingredients

2-3 cups vanilla yogurt, frozen
2-3 cups milk
1 tsp crushed peppermint candies
1 cup ice cubes

Preparation

Add the ingredients in a blender and blend them well. If you want to pulverize the peppermint candies then blend for a longer time. When you get your desired consistency, serve the smoothie. You can also use sprigs of peppermint to garnish the smoothie.Enjoy!

Broccoli and Spinach Smoothie

Ingredients

1 sized carrot, chopped
4-5 broccoli florets
1 sprig Spinach
1 apple, chopped
2-3 oranges
½ cup Water

Preparation

The fruits can be changed according to your taste. All the fruits and vegetables should be peeled and sliced. Take all the ingredients to a blender and blend them until a creamy texture is formed. Serve the delicious smoothie. Enjoy!

Ginger Coconut Smoothie

Ingredients

½ cup citrus Kombucha
1 cup ice cubes
2-3 tablespoon coconut butter
1 cup Pineapples cut into pieces
¼ tsp ginger powder

Preparation

Take a blender, add the ingredients to it and blend well. Blend until you get the desired texture. Delicious smoothie is ready to be served Enjoy!

Plum and Blueberry Smoothie

Ingredients

1 cup frozen blueberries
1 cup Red plums, pitted and cut into pieces
2 cups Greek yogurt
1 tsp Lemon juice extract

Preparation

Add all ingredients in a blender blend, gradually increase in the speed. When you get the desired texture, the healthy and delicious plum and berry smoothie is ready to be served. Enjoy!

Carrot-Apple Smoothie

This smoothie helps your skin glow since it has antioxidant properties.

Ingredients

1 cup carrot
1 cup apple

1 cup Ice cubes

Preparation

The carrot and apple taken can be either fresh or frozen. Blend the carrots and apples in a blender with the ice cubes and can also add sugar if desired. Blend them until a creamy texture is made. The smoothie is prepared to be served for breakfast.Enjoy!

Kiwi-Strawberry Smoothie

Ingredients

1 cup strawberries frozen or fresh
1 kiwi, peeled
2-3 tsp sugar
Ice cubes

Preparation

Add all ingredients into the blender and add sugar, if desired. Blend until a creamy consistency is achieved. Enjoy!

Cherry-Vanilla smoothie

Ingredients

1 ½ cup cherries, pitted
1 ¼ cup milk, low fat
2-3 tablespoon sugar
1 tsp Vanilla essence and Almond extract
Salt, to taste
Ice cube

Preparation

Add all ingredients to a blender until it forms a thick creamy consistency.Enjoy!

Apple and Oats Smoothie

Ingredients

2 apples, peeled and cut into cubes
1 cup Rolled oats
2 cups of rice milk
1 tsp honey
¼ tsp cinnamon powder

Preparation

Soak oats in rice milk for about 5-10 minutes. Now add all the ingredients to the blender and blend them wellEnjoy!

Pineapple and Mango Smoothie

Ingredients

1 cup Pineapple
1 cup Mango
½ cup Yogurt
1 cup Orange juice
½ tsp Honey
4-5 Ice cubes

Preparation

Cut the mangoes and the pineapples the night freeze. Now add all the ingredients to the blender and blend them gradually increasing the speed. Blend them until they get your desired texture. Enjoy!

Banana Crunch Smoothie

This is a low fat and low carb smoothie that is ideal if you are on a diet.

Ingredients

Banana, peeled
½ cup milk- low fat
1 tsp sugar-free honey
1 cup granola cereal
5 Ice cubes

Preparation

Take all the ingredients to the blender and blend them until you get your desired texture. When the needed consistency is achieved, the delicious and healthy smoothie is ready to be served. Enjoy!

Pineapple and Banana Smoothie

Ingredients

1 cup Pineapple juice
1 Banana, peeled and cut into pieces
1 cup Strawberries
1 tsp Vanilla essence
1 cup Vanilla yogurt

Preparation

Take all the ingredients to the blender, you can also add honey if you want added sweetness and blend them gradually at high speed until they attain a smooth texture. Enjoy!

Healthy Berry Smoothie

Ingredients

- 1 cup strawberries, blueberries and blackberries
- 1 scoop Whey powder,
- 2 tsp Flax seed oil
- 2 tsp Flax seeds
- 2 tbs Lemon juice,
- ½ cup Cranberry juice
- A pack of stevia
- Ice cubes (optional)
- 1 cup Water

Preparation

Add all the ingredients to a blender and blend them slowly until they get a smooth creamy texture. Enjoy!

No-fat Fruit Smoothie

Ingredients

- 1 cup apples cut in to pieces
- 2 bananas peeled and sliced
- 1 orange, peeled
- 1 tsp Honey, optional
- ½ cup ice cubes

Preparation

Add all the ingredients in a blender and blend them, gradually increase the speed until it is smooth. When the desired texture is attained, leave the smoothie for few minutes to give a good blend and then serve it. Enjoy!

Raspberry Lime Smoothie

Ingredients

- 3 tsp lime, juice
- ½ cup milk low fat
- ½ cup lime sherbet
- ½ cup raspberry
- ½ cup of ice

Preparation

Add all the ingredients to a blender and blend, until the desired texture is formed. When you get the desired consistency, your delicious raspberry and lime smoothie is ready to be served. If anyone does not have the lime sherbet, Enjoy!

Tropical Berry Tofu Smoothie

Ingredients

2 cup vanilla yogurt low fat or fat free
1 cup milk low fat or skimmed
1 cup Soft tofu, cut into small cubes

1 large banana
½ cup blueberries
1 cup strawberries

Preparation

Add all the ingredients to a blender and blend well until you get the desired creamy consistency. Begin blending slowly and gradually increase the speed. When the desired texture is received, serve it. Enjoy!

Banana Orange Smoothie

Ingredients

1 cup unsweetened vanilla yogurt
½ cup fat free milk
1 cup unsweetened orange juice

1 medium sized banana
1 cup ice cubes

Preparation

Add all the ingredients to a blender and blend them, until the desired creamy texture is formed. This can take up to 5-6 minutes. When blended well, the smoothie is ready to serve. Enjoy!

Yogurt Fruit Smoothie

Ingredients

2 cups vanilla yogurt
1 large banana
1 cup strawberries

½ tsp vanilla essence
½ tsp Lemon juice
1 cup Ice cubes,

Preparation

Cut and add bananas and the strawberries in the blender and blend them well until desired creamy consistency is achieved. Enjoy!

Raspberry Strawberry Smoothie

Ingredients

1 cup raspberry yogurt low fat
½ cup milk or cream

1 cup strawberries
1 cups ice cubes

Preparation

Add all the ingredients in a blender and blend well, until the desired consistency is formed. Once you get the creamy texture, the delicious raspberry strawberry smoothie is ready to be served. This smoothie has a high nutritional value as well and also provides energy. Enjoy!

Strawberry Blueberry and Banana Smoothie

Ingredients

For the Red layer
1 cup Strawberries
½ banana
1 cup vanilla milk
2 tbs crushed Ice

For the White layer
1 Banana

1 cup Vanilla milk
2 tsp Honey
2 tbs crushed Ice

For the Blue layer
1 cup Blueberries
½ cup Acai juice
2 tbs crushed Ice

Preparation

Add the ingredients mentioned under red layer and blend them well, pour in a glass and keep it in the freezer. Now blend the ingredients mentioned under white layer and pour them on the top of the red layer and finally repeat the same procedure with the blue layer, Serve Chilled Enjoy!

Blueberry Acai Berry Smoothie

Ingredients

1 cup blueberries
1 pack of pure acai berry puree

1 cup mango juice
1 cup Ice cubes, smashed

Preparation

Add all the ingredients to a blender and blend well. This When you get the desired creamy smoothie consistency, the amazingly tasted smoothie is ready to be served. Enjoy!

Purple Detox Smoothie

Ingredients

2-3 cups of acai juice
1 cup almond milk or soy milk 1 tsp soy creamer
1 cup blueberries

½ cup raspberries
1 large banana
1 tsp whole grain flaxseed meal
Ice cubes, smashed

1 tbs of macro greens powder
½ tsp. apple cider vinegar

½ tsp Cayenne powder

Preparation
All the fruits taken should be frozen. Add all the ingredients to the blender and blend well. Serve. Enjoy!

Blueberry Banana Smoothie, with Fax Seeds

Ingredients
1 cup blueberries
1 large sized banana
1 cup low-fat yogurt
½ cup artificially sweetened almond low fat milk
1 tsp of powered flax seeds
½ cup ice cubes

Preparation
Add all the ingredients to a blender and blend it at a low speed and gradually increase the speed, until the ingredients are smooth and the desired texture is formed. Leave the blender for some time and then serve it. Enjoy!

Gluten-Free Berry Smoothie

Ingredients
½ cup gluten free oatmeal
4-5 tsp orange juice concentrated
¾ cup vanilla yogurt
1 cup Blueberries 1 cup Strawberries
½ cup artificially sweetened vanilla almond milk

Preparation
Grind the oatmeal in a blender, until you get a fine texture of it. Now add all the ingredients to the blender and blend them well until you get the desired consistency from it. Enjoy!

Chocolate Banana smoothie

Ingredients
1 large banana
½ cup milk low fat
4-5 dates
1 tsp cocoa powder

Preparation
Add all the ingredients in a blender and blend till it gets a smooth texture. When you get the creamy texture, the delicious smoothie is ready to be served for your breakfast. This smoothie can also be had by people who are health conscious as the ingredients used are low on fat. Enjoy!

Healthy Heart Smoothie

Ingredients
1 cup strawberries
½ medium sized banana
1 cup vanilla yogurt low fat
½ cup raw almonds
½ cup oats
1 tsp of maple syrup

Preparation
Add all the ingredients in a blender and blend them, Enjoy!

Wheat Germ Smoothie

Ingredients
1 cup strawberries
½ a banana
1 cup vanilla yogurt low fat
5 Ice cubes
½ cup skimmed milk
1-2 tsp maple syrup

Preparation
Blend all ingredients in a blender and gradually increase the speed. Enjoy!

Sunup Smoothie

Ingredients
½ cup low fat or skim milk
½ cup strawberries
½ large banana
1 tsp protein powder
1 tsp wheat germ
1 tsp brewers' yeast

Preparation
Add all the ingredients in a blender and blend them until you get the desired creamy smooth texture. When you get the desired consistency, the delicious and healthy smoothie is ready to be served. Enjoy!

Protein Rich smoothie

Ingredients
1 cup unsweetened pomegranate juice
½ cup soy or almond milk, low fat
5 Ice cubes
1 Banana
1 tsp silver almonds
1 tsp Protein powder
Honey (optional)

Preparation

Add all the ingredients in a blender and blend until the creamy texture of the smoothie is formed. When you get the desired consistency, the delicious and healthy smoothie is ready to be served. Enjoy!

Low Carb Smoothie

Ingredients

1 small banana
2 cups Mixed fruits; strawberries, blueberries and available seasonal fruits

1 cup fruit juice, (any)
2-3 tsp coconut oil
1 scoop whey protein

Preparation

Add all the ingredients in a blender and blend well until a smooth, creamy texture is formed. When the desired texture of the smoothie is formed, the delicious and healthy smoothie is ready to be served. Enjoy!

Chocolate and Peanut butter- Banana Smoothie

Ingredients

cup chocolate coconut milk
1 large banana
tsp powdered peanut butter

1-2 tsp protein powder
½ avocado

Preparation

Add all the ingredients in a blender and blend slowly, until the desired creamy texture of the smoothie is formed. This smoothie is a great choice for breakfast, especially after a long and intense session of workout. Enjoy!

Peanut Butter and Oatmeal Smoothie

Ingredients

1 large banana, frozen
2-3 tsp rolled oats
2 tablespoons of peanut butter

½ cup almond milk
½ cup ice cubes

Preparation

Add all the ingredients in a blender and blend them thoroughly. When the desired consistency of the smoothie is ready, then serve cold

Orange and Melon Smoothie

Ingredients

1 cup honeydew, sliced and frozen
1 orange, peeled
½ cup low fat vanilla yogurt
½ tsp lemon juice
1 tsp honey
5 Ice cubes

Preparation

Add all the ingredients in a blender and blend until you get the desired creamy texture. Enjoy!

Tomato Smoothie

Ingredients

2 cups tomatoes, sliced
½ cup tomato juice
½ cup apple juice
½ cup Carrots chopped
¼ cup celery
Ice cubes

Preparation

Add all the ingredients in a blender and combine them together. Blend them till the creamy texture of the smoothie is achieved, the healthy and delicious smoothie is ready to be served for your breakfast. Enjoy!

Watermelon and Strawberry Smoothie

Ingredients

2-3 cups watermelon
1 cup cantaloupe
½ cup strawberries
1 cup yogurt low fat
1 cup ice cubes

Preparation

Add the ingredients to a blender and blend them well and gradually increase the speed. When the desired texture of the smoothie is formed, the healthy and delicious smoothie is ready to be served. This smoothie is a favourite among children Enjoy!

Limey Watermelon Smoothie

Ingredients

1 ½ cup watermelons chopped
1 ½ cup honeydew melon
1 Lime juice, unsweetened
1 cup vanilla yogurt low fat
1 cup ice cubes

Preparation

Add all the ingredients in a blender and blend them well until the desired consistency is made. This smoothie is low on calories Enjoy!

Cherry Cantaloupe Smoothie

Ingredients

1 cup cantaloupe, peeled and sliced
½ cup apple juice (you may also use apricot juice)
1 cup Cherries, pitted
1 cup Raspberries or Blackberries
1 cup ice cubes

Preparation

Add the ingredients in a blender and blend them well until the ingredients become smooth. When the desired texture is formed, serve the delicious smoothie in your breakfast. Enjoy!

Berry Healthy Smoothie Recipe

Ingredients

½ cup blueberries
½ cup Strawberries or Blackberries
1 medium sized carrot
1 cup skimmed milk1 cup pomegranates
1 cup ice cubes

Preparation

Blend all the ingredients in a blender until a smooth consistency is achieved. Enjoy!

Classic Green Detox Smoothie With Kale

Ingredients

4-5 Kale leaves
1 apple
1 banana
1 tsp ginger powder½ cup water

Preparation

Add all the ingredients in a blender, and blend them until the ingredients are thoroughly mixed and a creamy texture is formed. This easy to make smoothie can be enjoyed during breakfast. Enjoy!

Simple Smoothie Detox

Ingredients

1 Red grapefruit
1 Apple
1 banana
1 cup dandelion greens
½ cup water

Preparation

Add all the ingredients in a blender and blend them well until the texture is desirable. Serve chilled. Enjoy!

Rise and Shine Smoothie

Ingredients

½ cup low fat milk1 cup strawberries
1 Banana
1 tsp protein powder
1 tsp wheat germ
1 tsp yeast

Preparation

Add all the ingredients to a blender and blend them well. After blending them well, give it a standing time of few minutes and then serve. Have this healthy smoothie for breakfast. Enjoy!

Ruby Red Grapefruit Smoothie

Ingredients

½ cup water
2 large bananas
1 tsp flax seeds, powered
1 kiwi
2 Red grapefruits
2 cups baby spinach leaves

Preparation

Add all the ingredients in a blender and blend the ingredients together until a creamy texture is formed, if you think the smoothie has become thicker, then add a little more water to the blender and again mix them together. When they are thoroughly mixed, the smoothie is ready to be served. Enjoy!

Cherry Lemon Buzz Smoothie

Ingredients

1 cup cherries
½ cup Orange juice
1 Lemon juice
½ cup water
1-2 tsp honey,

Preparation

Add cherries, orange juice, and lemon juice in a blender and blend well by pouring the water gradually. Now open the lid of the blender and pour honey in it and blend again for a few minutes. Once you get the desired texture it is ready to be served. Enjoy!

Protein Power Smoothie

Ingredients

1 ½ cup strawberries frozen or fresh
1 cup orange juice
1 tsp protein powder
1-2 tsp flax seed oil
1 tsp yeast

Preparation

Add all the ingredients in a blender and blend till they form a creamy texture. Serve chilled. Enjoy!

Heart Healthy Oats and Fruit Smoothie

Ingredients

½ cup strawberries, either frozen or fresh
1 medium sized banana
½ cup almonds
½ cup rolled oats
1-2 tsp maple syrup

Preparation

Add all the ingredients in a blender and blend them, gradually increase the rate of speed to high. Enjoy!

Berry Banana smoothie

Ingredients

1 cup soy milk
1 cup mixed berries like strawberries, blueberries or blackberries
1 Banana
2-3 tsp protein powder

Preparation

Add all the ingredients in the blender and then blend them. When blended as desired, serve. Enjoy!

Blackberry and Peach Smoothie

Ingredients

½ cup blackberries
2 Peaches, cored
1 cup Low fat milk
1 cup ice cubes
Honey

Preparation

Add all the ingredients in a blender and blend them well until you get the desired texture. Once you get the texture this yummy smoothie is ready to be served. Enjoy!

Berry Fruit Smoothies

Ingredients

½ cup Low-fat lemon yogurt
1 cup dark sweet cherries frozen (pitted,)
1 cup vanilla soya milk low fat
½ cup blueberries, frozen
1 tsp lemonade concentrate,

Preparation

Put all the blue berries, frozen cherries in the blender. Now add soya milk and all the other ingredients and blend it well until the mixture turns smooth. Enjoy!

Green Smoothie

Ingredients

1 cup green grapes, frozen
¾ cup vanilla yogurt
2 cups pineapple chunks (frozen unsweetened)
1 cup firmly-packed baby spinach
2 cups natural unsweetened organic pineapple juice
1 tsp chocolate hazelnut spread

Preparation

Rinse the baby spinach and blend them along with other ingredients till a smooth and creamy consistency is formed. Enjoy!

365 Days of Smoothie Recipes

Sunrise Smoothies

Ingredients

½ cup concentrate orange juice
1 cup vanilla soy milk
1 medium banana
½ cup vanilla yogurt
1 tsp honey
1 cup ice cubes

Preparation

Add all the ingredients in a blender and blend until a rich creamy consistency is achieved. Serve chilled. Enjoy.

Orange Creamsicle Smoothies

Ingredients

1 11 oz. can mandarin oranges in juice, chilled
½ cup yogurt (vanilla or vanilla soy yogurt)
½ cup frozen pineapple chunks
1 Tsp. honey
1 cup vanilla soy milk
½ cup ice

Preparation

Preparation Blend the frozen juice and pineapple chunks well in blender now add all the remaining ingredients and blend till a smooth consist is achieved. Enjoy!

Strawberry Smoothie

Ingredients

2 cups frozen unsweetened strawberries
2 fresh strawberries for garnish
½ cup cranberry raspberry juice
¼ cup orange juice
½ cup vanilla yogurt

Preparation

Wash the strawberries and cranberry well before Preparation. Add the frozen strawberry in blender and make in smooth. Add the yogurt and all the juices in a blender and blend it again. Garnish with strawberries and serve chilled Enjoy!

Berry Blast Smoothie

Ingredients

- 2 cups baby spinach
- 2 cups frozen mixed berries (strawberries, raspberries, blackberries, blueberries and cherries)
- 1 cup plain Greek yogurt
- 1 tablespoon honey
- 1 cup milk, low fat or soy, almond or coconut milk

Preparation

Rinse the berries and spinach and blend them in a blender with other ingredients until a smooth consistency is achieved. Serve chilled. Enjoy!

Pineapple Coconut Smoothie

Ingredients

- 2 cups unsweetened pineapple chunks (frozen)
- ½ cup pineapple juice
- ½ cup coconut milk
- 1 tsp unsweetened shredded coconut
- ½ cup vanilla yogurt
- 1 tsp. honey
- 1 tsp pineapple chunks for garnish

Preparation

Use a blender to make the smoothie. Add pineapple chunks and pineapple juice and mix it well. Add the remaining ingredients and churn well. Serve chilled. Enjoy!

Banana Smoothie

Ingredients

- 1 large bananas
- 1 cup low-fat banana yogurt
- 1 cup frozen unsweetened pineapple chunks
- 1 ½ cup unsweetened pineapple juice 1 cup ice cubes
- A pinch of cinnamon powder for garnish

Preparation

Blend the bananas in a blender and with banana yogurt till it gets mixed well. Add the pineapple chunks and pineapple chunks next, and blend it again with the ice. Now pour the smoothie in serving glasses and garnish it well with cinnamon. Serve. Enjoy!

Watermelon Smoothie

Ingredients

2 cups watermelon, chopped and de-seeded
1 cup milk
1 tsp maple syrup
½ cup vanilla yogurt

Preparation

Add all the ingredients in a blender and churn well. Serve chilled. Enjoy!

Chocolate Banana Smoothie

Ingredients

2 large bananas
1 cup vanilla soy milk
¼ cup vanilla yogurt, low fat
1 tsp chocolate hazelnut spread
5-6 Ice cubes

Preparation

Add all the ingredients in a blender and churn well. Serve chilled. Enjoy!

Blueberry Fruit Smoothies

Ingredients

½ cup unsweetened pineapple chunks (frozen)
1-½ cups unsweetened blueberries (frozen)
1 cup pineapple juice
¾ cup lemon yogurt

Preparation

Place the pineapple chunks in smoothie blender and blend it first, now add the blueberries in it with the pineapple juice and blend it well, till it is smooth. Finally add lemon yogurt and blend. Pour the smoothie in serving glasses and serve chilled. Enjoy!

Peach Smoothie

Ingredients

2 cups peaches, chopped
½ cup vanilla soy milk
½ cup pineapple juice
¼ cup low-fat vanilla yogurt
5-6 Ice cubes

Preparation

Peel and slice the peaches carefully rinse them. Now place the peaches in smoothie maker or blender and blend it with pineapple juice. now add soy milk and yogurt in it. Blend it well. Pour the smoothie in serving glasses and add some crushed ice. Enjoy!

Chocolate Strawberry Smoothies

Ingredients

- 2 cups frozen strawberries
- 2 tsp. chocolate chips
- ½ cup pineapple juice
- ½ cup vanilla yogurt non-fat
- 1 tsp. unsweetened cocoa powder

Preparation

Add all the ingredients in a blender and churn well. Serve chilled. Enjoy!

Pumpkin Smoothies

Ingredients

- ½ cup pumpkin puree
- ½ tsp. pumpkin pie spice
- ¾ cup pineapple chunks frozen
- 1 cup orange juice
- 1 tsp. brown sugar
- ½ cup vanilla yogurt
- 1 cup whole graham cracker
- A pinch of cinnamon powder for garnish

Preparation

Pour pumpkin puree, with pumpkin pie spice in a blender add pineapple chunks and blend until smooth. Then add orange juice, brown sugar and yogurt and blend it well with graham crackers once the smoothie is prepared pour the same in serving glasses and garnish it with cinnamon powder. Serve chilled. Enjoy!

Mixed fruit Smoothie

Ingredients

- 1 cup ice cubes
- 2 cup strawberries
- 1 banana
- 1 cup blueberries
- 1 cup milk
- A dash of vanilla syrup
- Cocoa powder for garnish

Preparation

The base of this drink is ice so place the same in blender and crush it well. When the crushed ice is ready add strawberries and banana with the blueberries on it and blend it again. Add the milk and vanilla syrup on it and blend it again. Pour it in serving glasses when the smoothie is ready, sprinkle some cocoa powder and garnish. Serve chilled Enjoy!

Pomegranate Berry Smoothie

Ingredient

2 cups Pomegranate and berries frozen
1 cup pomegranate - berries juice
1 Medium sized banana
½ cup cottage cheese of no fat
½ cup water
½ cup milk (no fat, optional)

Preparation

Combine all ingredients in a blender and blend well until a rich and creamy consistency is achieved. Serve chilled. Enjoy!

Cantaloupe Smoothie

Ingredients

1 banana
¼ ripe cantaloupes coarsely chopped and de-seeded.
½ cup yogurt low-fat
2 tsp dry milk, no fat1
½ concentrate frozen orange juice
1 tsp honey
½ tsp vanilla extract

Preparation:

Add all ingredients in a blender and churn well. Serve chilled. Enjoy!

PB&J Smoothie

Ingredients

2 cups Strawberries chopped (fresh or frozen)
1 Banana frozen, chopped
2 cups Greek yogurt
1 tsp smooth peanut butter Ice ½ cup

Preparation

Combine all ingredients in a blender and blend well until a rich and creamy consistency is achieved. Serve chilled. Enjoy!

Tropical Morning Smoothie

Ingredients

1 cup plain Greek yogurt
½ cup fresh pineapple chunks
½ cup fresh or frozen mango chunks 2 tsp flax seeds

1 chopped frozen banana

Preparation

Combine all ingredients in a blender and blend well until a rich and creamy consistency is achieved. Serve chilled. Enjoy!

Honeydew-Kiwifruit Smoothie

Ingredients

1 kiwifruit
1 tsp lemon juice
1 cup honeydew and/or kiwifruit slices
1 small Granny Smith apple
3 tsp sugar
1 cup ice cubes

Preparation

Combine all ingredients in a blender and blend well until a rich and creamy consistency is achieved. Serve chilled. Enjoy!

Apple Sangria Smoothie

Ingredients

2 red apples
2 oranges
juice of 1 lime
1 cup white-grape juice, chilled

Preparation

Make orange juice from extracting the juice from 10 oranges and extract the apple juice with the same way from 16 apples and lemon juice from 6 lemons. At least, 2 quarts of apple juice for this preparation. Slice rest of the apple and the orange also in thinly size. Stir it with orange juice and keep the mixture in chilling temperature. Add grape juice and the fruits after the fruits before serving. Enjoy!

Pomegranate Berry Smoothie

Ingredients

2 cups whole Pomegranate berries frozen
1 cup pomegranate berries juice
1 medium sized banana
½ cup - cottage cheese no fat
½ cup water
½ cup milk (optional)

Preparation

Combine all ingredients in a blender and make a thick smooth concoction. Serve chilled. Enjoy!

Cantaloupe Smoothie

Ingredients

1 Banana
1 ¼ ripe cantaloupe, coarsely chopped and de-seeded.
1 ½ yogurt no fat
Tsp milk no fat 2 ½ concentrate frozen orange juice 2 tsp honey
½ tsp vanilla bean extract tsp

Preparation

Combine all ingredients in a blender and make a thick smooth concoction. Serve chilled. Enjoy!

Green Smoothie with Kefir

Ingredients

1 cup plain kefir 1 small beet
1 large carrot
1 cup spinach
1 small apple 1 banana ripped
½ half avocado
½ cup mixed fresh berries
1 small peach

Preparation

Combine all ingredients in a blender and make a thick smooth concoction. Serve chilled. Green Smoothie with Kefir is excellent source of calcium for your strong bones and source of protein for your structure strong muscles. Enjoy!

Green Smoothie with Spinach Banana Berries

Ingredients

1 cup frozen Berries
1 ripe banana
1 cup organic baby spinach
½ cup ice water

Preparation

Combine all ingredients in a blender and make a thick smooth concoction. Serve chilled. Serves as a perfect smoothie for lunch. Enjoy!

Freckled PB&J

Ingredients
½ cup vanilla soymilk
1 cup red grapes
1 scoop vanilla protein powder

½ cup creamy peanut butter
1 cup crushed ice

Preparation
Combine all ingredients in a blender and make a thick smooth concoction. Serve chilled Enjoy!

Berry Good Smoothie

Ingredients
1 ¾ cup milk
1 scoop vanilla protein powder

2 cups frozen mixed berries of.

Preparation
First combine all ingredients until creamy. Creamy smoothies make the perfect summertime dessert. Mix ice cream together, frozen mixed berries, and whole milk for a healthy to beat the heat. Enjoy!

Frog Juice Smoothie

Ingredients
450 grams canned pineapple juice
1 ¾ cup greens *(organic Super greens)
1 ripe mango

1 ripe banana
1 ice cubes

Preparation
Combine all ingredients in a blender and make a thick smooth concoction. Serve chilled Enjoy!

Peanut Butter Cup Smoothie

Ingredients
1 cup TruMoo chocolate milk
¼ cup creamy peanut butter
1 scoop chocolate flavor vitamin powder

¾ cup crushed ice
½ cup avocado

Preparation
Combine all ingredients in a blender and make a thick smooth concoction. Serve chilled Enjoy!

Blueberry Cheesecake Smoothie

Ingredients

1 cup vanilla soymilk of
½ cup fresh blueberries
¼ cup graham crackers

114 grams honey flavored Greek yogurt
1 frozen banana
¾ cup crushed ice

Preparation

Combine all ingredients in a blender and make a thick smooth concoction. Serve chilled Your delicious, healthy smoothie is ready.Enjoy!

Tea for Two Smoothie

Ingredients

1 cup brewed caffeine of free Match Green Tea
¼ cup soymilk

½ cup vanilla yogurt
½ cup crushed ice

Preparation

First prepare tea and let it be breezy. Then add yogurt, tea and milk in a food processor blend until smooth now add crushed ice. and blend again. Tea for Two Smoothie is great source of calcium and protein. Enjoy!

Apple Crisp Smoothie

Ingredients

¾ cup apple juice
½ brae burn apple cored
1 scoop vanilla protein powder

½ cup frozen baby carrots
114 grams vanilla flavored Greek yogurt of
½ cup oatmeal, uncooked

Preparation

Combine all ingredients in a blender and make a thick smooth concoction. Serve chilledEnjoy!

Cream Smoothie

Ingredients

1 cup orange juice
½ cup milk
½ cup orange sherbet

170 grams vanilla yogurt

Emma Katie

Preparation

Combine all ingredients in a blender and make a thick smooth concoction. Serve chilled Enjoy!

Avocado-Pear Smoothie

Ingredients

1 unit mellow Hass avocado ½ cup Greek yogurt no fat

1 cup pear juice 2 tsp honey ½ tsp vanilla extract
1 cup ice cubes

Preparation:

Combine all ingredients in a blender and make a thick smooth concoction. Serve chilled Enjoy!

Banana and Kiwi Smoothie

Ingredients

1 banana, chopped
1 kiwi chopped
1 cup yogurt low fat

½ cup ice cubes
1 tsp maple syrup

Preparation

Combine all ingredients in a blender and make a thick smooth concoction. Serve chilled Enjoy!

Yogurt-Pistachio Smoothies

Ingredients

2 cups plain yogurt (fresh preferred)
½ cup of water
1 ½ tsp ginger fine chopped
½ cup pistachios (salted)

¼ tsp pepper powder
1 cup ice cubes
¼ cup fine chopped pistachios

Preparation

Add yogurt, fresh water, chopped ginger to add a dash of spice, salted pistachios, pepper powder, ice cubes into a blender and blend it until smooth. Pour the smoothie into glasses and garnish with fine chopped pistachios. Enjoy!

Fruit Smoothie

Ingredients

2 navel (seedless) oranges, peeled and pitted cut into chunks

1 cup frozen raspberries
1 cup frozen blueberries

Preparation

Combine all ingredients in a blender and make a thick smooth concoction. Serve chilled Enjoy!

Strawberry, Mango, and Yogurt Smoothie

Ingredients

1 ¼ cups apple juice (other fruit juices are also fine)
1 cup l plain yogurt low fat

1 cup strawberries
2 cups mango chunks

Preparation

Add all the fruits and juices into a blender and blend until smooth, Enjoy!

Banana, Oat and Fig Smoothie

Ingredients

1 banana,
2-3 dried figs
½ cup oats s

1 cup milk 2 tsp honey
¼ cup almonds

Preparation

Combine all ingredients in a blender and make a thick smooth concoction. Serve chilled Enjoy!

Creamy Date Smoothie

Ingredients

½ cup milk
5-6 dates, pitted

5-6 Ice cubes

Preparation

Blend all ingredients in a food processor until smooth. Serve chilled. Enjoy!

Banana Apricot and Mango smoothie

Ingredients
1 banana
2 ripe mangoes
1 cup yoghurt or apple juice
2 dried apricots

Preparation
Combine all ingredients in a blender and make a smoothie, Adjust the speed of the blender depending upon the smoothness of the mixture. Then keep on blending it till its smooth. If you wish to dilute it, you may add water, juice or some milk. Enjoy!

Banana and Strawberry Smoothies

Ingredients
1 cup strawberries
1 cup ripe bananas
1 cup yoghurt, vanilla flavor
1 cup Milk

Preparation
Combine all ingredients in a blender and make a smooth paste. Add water to dilute the consistency if desired. Enjoy!

Spiced Pumpkin Smoothie

Ingredients
1 cup pumpkin puree
1 cup ice cubes
1 cup milk
½ tsp Powered nutmeg
1 tsp honey

Preparation
Add the pure pumpkin puree with the milk and the ice cubes. Then pour the milk and the honey to the puree. Start blending at a till smooth. If in case you do not get the pure pumpkin puree, you can substitute it with pumpkin pie filling. In that case you can skip the nutmeg and the honey. Serve the smoothie in tall glasses. Enjoy!

Banana and Berry Smoothie

Ingredients

½ cup banana
1 cup mixed berries, preferably raspberries or blueberries, frozen
1 cup Milk
1 tsp Honey

Preparation

Cut bananas into fine pieces. Then add the frozen berries along with the milk and the honey into a blender. Blend until smooth. You may add some more honey If desired. The berries if soaked in milk for a long time can make the blending process faster. Also, you may change the thickness of the smoothie by adding some more milk or water Enjoy!

Peach, Pear and Fresh Ginger Smoothies

Ingredients

1 cup pear juice
1 cup peaches 1 tsp fresh ginger chopped
1 cup Greek yoghurt
1 banana

Preparation

Combine all ingredients in a blender and blend until smooth. Serve chilled. Enjoy!

Strawberry and Mango Smoothie

Ingredients

1 cup Sara Lee fresh strawberries (frozen)
1 cup thawed mangoes
1 tsp honey
1 cup milk
1 cup yoghurt, preferably vanilla flavored
1 cup crushed ice

Preparation

Firstly, add the frozen strawberries and the thawed mangoes in a blender jar. Gradually increase the speed of the blender to make the mixture smooth, add the milk, honey and the vanilla flavored yoghurt in the mixture. Try this entire procedure with half of the constituents. After blending, serve the smoothie in two chilling glasses. Now, repeat the same process with the rest of the ingredients. Enjoy!

Collard Green Lime and Mango Smoothie

Ingredients
2 cups Fresh lime juice
1 cup collard greens (chopped and stemmed, you may also use spinach)
1 cup Frozen mango
1 cup Green grapes

Preparation
Combine all ingredients in a blender and blending until smooth. Enjoy!

Raspberry and Peach Smoothie

Ingredients
1 cup Peach slices (they can be canned or fresh peaches but in natural drained juice)
1 cup raspberries
2 cups fruit juice (any)
1 cup Vanilla yoghurt or vanilla ice cream
5-6 Ice cubes

Preparation
Add the fresh peach slices; raspberries and the fruit juice in a blender gradually blend all these into a single smooth puree. Add some ice cubes to it to make the smoothie chilling cool. Serve. Enjoy!

Orange - Cranberry Power Smoothie

Ingredients
1 cup cranberry juice
1 banana
1 orange, peeled
¼ protein powder
½ cup strawberries
¼ raspberry sherbet
1 cup ice cubes

Preparation
Firstly, blend the strawberries, banana, and orange, raspberry and protein powder along with some ice cubes for about one minute. The mixture needs to be strained for an easy flow through the straw. You can check the consistency of the sherbet and can add some sherbet or cranberry juice depending upon the thickness. Blend it again along with the previous one after you add more sherbet or cranberry juice. Serve this Enjoy!

Chocolate Strawberry Smoothie

Ingredients

2 bananas, chunked and one frozen
1 tsp of chocolate syrup

½ cup frozen strawberries
1 cup yogurt (plain)

Preparation:

In a blender add the bananas (both the chunked and the frozen one), the strawberries and the plain yogurt. Then add two tablespoons of chocolate syrup in the blender. Blend until smooth. You can check the consistency of the blended smoothie and add to the dilute by adding more yogurt to it. Continue blending until it turns smooth. Serve it in two glasses along with a straw. You can use a cherry to garnish it or even add ice cubes. Enjoy!

Banana and Peanut smoothie

Ingredients

1 banana sliced
1 cup chocolate milk low fat
½ cup milk
½ cup water

1 tsp brown sugar
½ cup peanuts butter
1 cup yogurt
1 cup vanilla cream

Preparation

Combine all ingredients together until smooth. Serve chilled. Enjoy!.

Blackberries Smoothie with Strawberries Toppings

Ingredients

1 cup blue berries
1 cup black berries
1 cup strawberries
2 cups vanilla ice cream

½ tsp brandy
5-6 ice cubes
1 tsp fresh cream

Preparation

Add black berries and blue berries in a blender and blend it well. Then add ice cubes, vanilla ice cream, and brandy and blend it again. Pour the mixture in a glass and garnish with some fresh cream on it. Then put some strawberries on it for garnishing. Serve chilled. Enjoy!

Kiwi Orange Smoothie

Ingredients

½ cup banana
½ cup strawberry
1 kiwi
1 cup vanilla ice cream
1 cup yogurt

½ cup pineapple juice
1 cup orange juice
Basil leaves for garnish
5-6 Ice cubes

Preparation

Add the sliced banana, strawberries and kiwi into the blender and mix it well. Then add some yogurt, vanilla ice cream and pineapple juice and mix it again. Pour the drink into a glass and mix some orange juice. garnish with basil leaves. Enjoy!

Strawberry Smoothie with Watermelon

Ingredients

½ cup watermelon
1 cup strawberries
1 cup yogurt
1 tsp brown sugar
1 scoop vanilla cream

¼ cup orange juice
4-5 mint leaves
Orange slices for garnishing
5-6 ice cubes

Preparation

Add watermelon slices, strawberries and brown sugar in a blender and blend it well. Then add some yogurt, orange juice and fresh vanilla cream and blend again. Pour in tall glassed and garnish with mint leaves and orange slices. Enjoy!

Neem-Lemon Smoothie

Ingredients

1 neem leave
2 cups water
½ cup lime juice
½ tsp refined salt
½ tsp brown sugar

5-6 ice cubes
1 Lemon slice
1 cup yogurt
1 cup orange juice

Preparation

Boil the neem leave with small amount of water and remove the leaves after boiling. Use this water, lemon juice, brown sugar, yogurts and orange juice in the blender and mix it well. Then pour the drink in a glass and garnish with a lemon ring. If the drink becomes bitter then add some lemon juice Serve chilled Enjoy!

Fresh Cream Fruit Smoothie

Ingredients

1 cups strawberries, chopped
1 banana
1 cup peaches, chopped
1 cup orange juice
1 cup mango juice
5-6 ice cubes
¼ cup chocolate chips
1 Tsp fresh cream

Preparation

Add strawberries, bananas, peaches and some ice cubes into the juicer and blend well. Then add some mango juice and orange juice and blend again. Add some ice cubes in a glass and keep it in the fridge for 30 minutes. When the glass becomes chilled pour the drink into the glass and garnish with some fresh cream on it. Also sprinkle some chocolate chips over it. Serve it chilled. Enjoy!

Green Mango Pepper Smoothie Ingredients

Ingredients

1 green mango
1 tsp pepper powder
5-6 ice cubes
¼ cup lemon juice
½ cup orange juice
1 lemon rinds
Salt, as per taste
1 tsp brown sugar
1 cup water

Preparation

Combine all ingredients in a blender except pepper powder and lemon ring, blend. Serve chilled and garnish with pepper powder and lemon ring. Enjoy!

Protein Enriched Strawberry Smoothie

Ingredients

1 cup milk low fat
1 cup yogurt
2 bananas
1 tsp protein supplements
1 tsp honey
1 cup strawberries, chopped
4 mint leaves
1 tsp brown sugar
1 cup vanilla ice cream

Preparation

Blend the yogurt and milk with the bananas in a blender. Add some salt. Then add brown sugar to make it sweet. After this, pour honey and add protein supplements in the mix. Add the strawberries, and garnish with mint leaves. While garnishing, first put the smoothie in a round-bottomed glass, and then put one scoop of vanilla ice cream on it. Enjoy!

Blueberry Peppermint Smoothie

Ingredients

2 cups blueberries
½ cup lemon juice
2-3 tsp sugar
Rock salt as per taste
1 apricot grated
mint leaves for garnish
¼ cup peppermint grated
1 cup ice cubes
1 cup fresh yogurt (sweet)
1 tsp Peppermint essence
2 tsp fresh cream for garnishing

Preparation

The blueberries should be de-seeded before putting them in the blender. Mix the blueberries with yogurt and make thick paste. Then add salt, sugar, mint leaves, and peppermint essence in the same mix in the blender. Add ice cubes; serve the smoothie in tall-necked glasses. Serve chilled with cream scoops. Enjoy!

Vodka-Cream Smoothie

Ingredients

1 tsp vodka
½ cup Fresh cream
1 bottle chilled soda
¼ cup raspy roasted almonds
1 sprig basil leaves
½ cup aerated drink
½ tsp refined salt
2-3 tsp refined sugar
Mint leaves for garnishing

Preparation

In a small glass, add fresh cream and the roasted almonds till it becomes a thick paste. Pour the aerated drink and layer on top and fill ¼ of the glass. Add salt, sugar and pour the chilled soda, please make sure that the layer of cream remains under the aerated drink. Then put some ice cubes, and basil leaves. Pour the vodka on top. Enjoy!

Carrot Smoothie

Ingredients

½ cup chopped carrot
1 tsp lemon juice
½ apple
2 tsp sugar
2 tsp fresh cream
5-6 ice cubes
1 sprig Basil leaves
½ cup water
1 ½ cup white soda

Preparation

Boil the carrot and discard the water after boiling. Then add the carrots, apple and sugar in a blender and blend well. Add some lemon juice, of some water and blend again. Then pour the drink it in a glass and add some soda. Add ice cubes and garnish with some fresh cream on it and basil leaves and a lemon rind on the top of the glass for garnishing. Serve chilled. Enjoy!

Chocolate Cookies with Ice-cream Smoothie

Ingredients

½ cup water
¼ cup Chocolate sauce
¼ cup chocolate chips
1 cup vanilla ice cream

5-6 ice cubes
1 tsp fresh cream
½ cup Milk
Chocolate powder for garnishing

Preparation

Mix the chocolate sauce, some water and milk in a juicer. Take a glass and spread some chocolate sauce inside the glass and put the mixture. Then add some vanilla ice cream and chocolate chips on the top of the smoothie. garnish with some fresh cream on and chocolate powder Serve chilled. Enjoy!

Banana-Chocolate Smoothie

Ingredients

1 banana, sliced
1-2 tsp chocolate sauce
1 cup milk
5-6 ice cubes

1 tsp fresh creams
1 cup vanilla ice cream
Chocolate chips for garnish

Preparation

Add the bananas, milk and vanilla ice cream in a blender and blend well. Then add chocolate sauce and ice cubes and blend again. Take a long glass and put the smoothie into the glass and spread some fresh cream in it. Put some chocolate chips on it for garnishing. Add some ice cubes and serve chilled. This is a healthy and delicious smoothie and it has low cholesterol and fat contains Enjoy!

Rainy day smoothie

Ingredients

1 mango sliced
1 sliced bananas
1 cup orange juice

1 cup vanilla flavored yogurt low fat
1 cup ice cubes
½ mango cubes

Preparation

Add sliced mango, bananas and yogurt into the juicer and mix it well. Then add some orange juice and vanilla low fat yogurt and mix it again. Take a short glass and pour the drink in it. Add some ice cubes. Add some mango cubes on it for garnishing. Mango is a very good source of vitamins and minerals and the orange juice provides anti-oxidants. Enjoy!

Coolers Smoothie Ingredients

1 cup sliced watermelon
1 cup ice cubes
1 tsp lemon juice
1 tsp sugar
½ tsp salt
½ cup water melon cubes for garnish

Preparation

De-seed the watermelon cubes and put them into the blender and mix it well. Then add some ice cubes and lemon juice and mix it for few seconds. Add sugar and salt and blend it again. Take a long stemmed glass and put the smoothie into the glass. Drizzle lemon juice on it. Add some ice cubes and garnish with water melon cubes. Enjoy!

Pumpkin Smoothie

Ingredients

½ cup bananas sliced
½ cup pumpkin cubes
1 cup milk
1 tsp refined sugar
½ tsp cinnamon powder
2 tsp fresh cream
2 scoops vanilla ice cream
½ cup ice cubes
½ tsp white vodka
2 tsp chocolate sauce
¼ cup Crushed peanuts

Preparation

Combine all ingredients together and blend well. Garnish with chocolate sauce. Enjoy!

Caramel Smoothie

Ingredients

1 tsp butter
1 tsp caramel essence
1 tsp caramelized,
 brown sugar for garnish
½ cup condensed milk
½ cup plain milk
1 -2 tsp sugar
2 tsp pistachio, grated for garnish

Preparation

Add milk and butter sugar in a Blend it until smooth. Fill ¼th of a long-stemmed glass with the mixture. Then pour caramelized brown sugar, and then fill the remaining 1/3rd glass with condensed milk. Then again add caramelized sugar. Garnish with grated pistachio. Enjoy!

Sweet Spinach Smoothie

Ingredients

½ cup blanched spinach
1 tsp refined brown sugar
A pinch cinnamon powder
3 flavoured wafer sticks

½ cup fresh sweet cream
1-2 tsp roasted almonds for garnishing
1 tsp milk powder
½ cup ice cubes

Preparation

Add the blanched spinach and sugar into the blender and make a fine paste. Take a round glass, and pour a thick layer of the mixture first. Then whip the sweet cream with cinnamon powder, and fill ¼th of the for the second layer. Then add milk powder, ice and roasted almonds on top for garnishing. Enjoy!

Pineapple Smoothie

Ingredients

1 cup pineapple slices
2 tsp pineapple essence
2 tsp peanut butter
1 cup condensed milk

2 tsp fresh cream
½ cup sugar granules
½ tsp salt Some crushed ice
2 Strawberry flavored wafers

Preparation

First add peanut butter, pineapple, cream, pineapple essence into the blender, and blend smoothly. Sieve the pineapple juice; take the pulp, and mix it with sugar and peanut butter for one more time in the blender. Then put it in a wide-mouthed glass, and fill up ¼th of the glass with this mixture. Then slowly pour condensed milk on top. Add crushed ice and dip the wafers into it. Enjoy!

Asparagus Smoothie

Ingredients

1 bundle Asparagus
1 bundle Grass shoots
1 cup fresh cream
1 tsp milk powder

Salt to taste

2 tsp refined brown sugar
½ cup water
Some crushed ice

Basil leaves for garnish
1 tsp mint essence

Preparation

Blend the asparagus and grass shafts inside a blender. Add a pinch of salt, and 2 tablespoons of refined brown sugar. Add less water to make it a thick paste. Then add the mint essence slightly as you pour the smoothie into a tall wine glass. You can also add basil leaves, crushed ice while blending serve chilled, Enjoy!

Deep Blue Smoothie

Ingredients

2 tsp blue edible syrup (use fruit syrup, without any preservative)
2 tsp sugar
½ tsp salt 1 tsp orange marmalade
4-5 Grated cherry, for garnishing

1 tsp vanilla essence
2 tsp cream
½ cup condensed milk
Some cashew nuts. grated for garnishing

Preparation

Blend the blue syrup with the condensed milk, in a blender. Make a smooth and thick mixture. Add salt and refined sugar to it, then add some vanilla essence, and fill ½ of a round-mouthed glass with this mixture. Add fresh cream as a second layer. Garnish with cherry and cashew nuts. Add one scope of orange marmalade on top. Enjoy!

Yogurt Smoothie

Ingredients

½ cup rose syrup
½ cup fresh sweet yogurt
1/3 cup refined castor sugar
Some rose petals for garnishing

4-5 dried saffron strands pinch of cardamom powder
1/3 cup condensed milk

Preparation

This smoothie is easy to make. Blend the yogurt, condensed milk and rose syrup in a blender, add fresh cream and blend it again. Add a pinch of cardamom powder, and pour the mixture into a glass. Add saffron strands and raised petals for garnishing. Make a layer with castor sugar on top, and then again add one dollop of condensed milk. Enjoy!

Apricot Delight

Ingredients

1 cup apricot kernel
2 tsp castor sugar
1 tsp salt
Some crushed ice

2 tsp peanut butter
2 tsp sweet frozen cream
1 tsp vanilla essence
½ cup hazelnut kernel

Preparation

First blend the apricot kernel, crushed ice, peanut butter, salt and sugar into the blender, and fill a full long-stemmed glass with this smooth concoction. Add vanilla essence, and make a layer with the hazelnut kernel. For the remaining mixture in the blender, add cream, whip it, and make a second layer on top. Add some fresh cream and hazelnut for garnishing. Enjoy!

Cappuccino Smoothie

Ingredients

1 tsp cappuccino powder
2 tsp brown refined sugar
½ cup chocolate sauce
½ cup chocolate cream biscuits, crushed

2 scoops chocolate ice cream
½ cup condensed milk
Some raisins for garnishing

Preparation

Blend coffee extract, brown sugar, condensed milk and raisins in a blender, and pour the smoothie in a tall glass. Fill half glass with this mixture, and then pour a thick layer of chocolate sauce on top. Add 2 scoops of chocolate ice creams as topping, and crushed cream biscuits for and raisins for garnishing. Serve chilled. Enjoy!

Corn-Oats and Barley Trio

Ingredients

½ cup boiled corn
½ cup boiled barley
½ cup boiled oats
1/3 cup refined sugar
1 tsp cola essence

Some fresh mint leaves
Some strawberry wafers
Some pistachio for garnishing
1 dollop of fresh cream

Preparation

Blend oats and corn in a blender. Add sugar, salt, cola essence, fresh cream and ice cubes and blend again into a smooth mix. Then fill half portion of a glass with this mixture, and add barley. Corn and barley should be separate layers. Garnish with strawberry wafers pistachio and cream. Enjoy!

Cabbage Smoothie

½ cup green cabbage, chopped
½ cup purple cabbage chopped
2 tsp castor sugar
1 tsp Salt
Pinch of cardamom powder
½ cup fresh cream
½ cup yogurt
4-5 ice cubes Shredded cabbage for garnishing

Preparation

For making this awesome vegan smoothie, first boil the green cabbages and blend them in a blender. Mix salt, sugar, yogurt, cardamom powder, ice cubes and fresh cream and pour it into a tall glass. (do not fill the glass). Make sure that the glass has been kept in the freezer for more than two hours. Blend the purple cabbages also in the similar manner and pour to in the glass to make a second layer. Garnish with shredded cabbage. Enjoy!

Golden Sun Smoothie

Ingredients

1 cup ripe papaya
½ cup fresh blueberry
½ cup condensed milk
1/3rd cup yogurt
2 tsp refined brown sugar
Salt as per taste
Some cherries for garnishing
Some grated papaya for garnishing

Preparation

Add ripe papaya pieces in a blender. Add condensed milk, fresh blueberries sugar, salt, and yogurt and crushed ice and blend it into a thick paste. Take a glass, and fill up more than half of the glass with this mixture. Pour condensed milk on top, and fill up the whole glass. Add blueberries, cherries, ice cubes and grated papaya for garnishing. Serve chilled. Enjoy!

Guava Smoothie

Ingredients

1 ripe guava
1 tsp salt 2 tsp refined brown sugar
1 tsp milk powder
Some crushed ice
Some Mint leaves
1 ½ cup aerated drink, cola, or orange soda
Crushed cashew nuts for garnishing

Preparation

First deseed the ripe guava, and add the pieces in a blender, then milk powder, salt, sugar mint leaves, and blend it again. The consistency should be thick. Now pour it in a tall glass, and let it settle. Then add cola or orange soda as a top layer. Garnish with cashew nuts. Enjoy!

Litchi Smoothie

Ingredients

1 cup litchi, de-seeded
2 tsp refined sugar granules
1 tsp salt
½ cup water
Some crushed ice

Basil leaves for garnishing
1 tsp cardamom powder
½ cup condensed milk
Raisins for garnishing

Preparation

First, blend the litchi with sugar, cardamom powder and crushed ice. Pour this mixture and fill up 1/3rd of a round glass. Add a layer of raisins. The add condensed milk in the rest of the mixture and blend it one more time. Add sugar and basil leaves on another layer, and fill the rest of the glass with the condensed milk mixture. Garnish with raisins and basil leaves. Enjoy!

Raspberry Smoothie

Ingredients

1 cup raspberry
1 tsp raspberry essence or syrup
2 tsp brown sugar granules
1 cup chocolate wafers
Some crushed ice

2 tsp fresh cream
½ cup fresh yogurt fat free
Mint leaves for garnish
A pinch of cinnamon powder

Preparation

First blend the raspberry into a blender, by adding sugar, sweet cream, crushed ice and yogurt in it. Then add 1 pinch of cinnamon powder and again blend the mixture. Add mint leaves, and put the mixture in a round-mouthed glass. Do not blend the mint leaves. Then put a layer of raspberry syrup on top. Garnish with 3 chocolate wafers. Enjoy!

Green Envy

Ingredients

1 cup gourd pulp
1/3 cup refined brown sugar
1 tsp salt 6 ice cubes
½ cup orange juice

1 tsp orange essence
Some mint leaves for garnishing
Grated gourd for topping

Preparation

Add the gourd pulp in a blender, add sugar and salt, and fill up a long-stemmed glass which has already been cooled in the freezer. Put the smoothie in it, and pour sufficient orange juice on top, to fill up the glass. Add orange essence and herbs for garnishing. Add grated gourd for garnishing. Serve it chilled. Enjoy!

Vegan Smoothie

Ingredients

½ cup carrot ½ cup beet
½ cup c vegan condensed milk or almond milk
1 tsp refined sugar
1 tsp carrot essence

1 tsp purple food color (edible)
Basil leaves for garnishing
Carrot wedge for garnishing
Shredded beet for topping
1 cup ice cubes

Preparation

Blend the carrot and the beets in the blender. Add salt, sugar, ice cubes and condensed milk, and blend it again. Then fill in a tall glass, with this smoothie. Place one carrot wedge on top, and pour some condensed milk as a top layer. Add purple food color, basil leaves, and shredded beet on top for garnishing. Serve it chilled with breakfast or snacks. Enjoy!

Brazilian Ginseng and Orange Smoothie

Ingredients

2-3 tsp brown refined sugar pellets
2 tsp orange marmalade
½ cup range extracts
1 cup orange juice

½ cup condensed sweet yogurt
Nuts for topping
Basil leaves for garnishing

Preparation

Blend the ginseng root and the basil leaves along with the orange extracts, and orange juice into the blender. Make sure that the ginseng roots blends properly. Then pour the condensed sweet yogurt into this mixture and pour this smoothie into a round glass. Add basil leaves, nuts, crushed ice and orange marmalade for topping. Enjoy!

Cool and exotic smoothie with cucumber and mint

Ingredients

½ cup cucumber
¼ cup mint leaves
1 tsp mint extract (sweet flavored)
1 tsp cucumber essence

2 tsp sugar
Salt as per taste
1 cup condensed milk
Cream for garnishing

Preparation

Add cucumber in the blender and mix well with mint leaves. It should be a smooth paste, and do not pour any water or ice. Instead, put sugar, condensed milk and fresh cream to it, and then blend it thoroughly. Pour the smoothie in a tall glass and garnish with cream, mint essence and cucumber essence. You can also use wafers for garnishing. Serve chilled. Enjoy!

Dried Berry Smoothie

Ingredients

1 cup pumpkin pulp
½ cup condensed milk
2 tsp cream
1 tsp fresh vanilla extract
¼ cup dried blackberry

2 tsp apricot kernel grated (for garnishing)
2-3 tsp refined brown sugar granules
1 tsp salt
½ cup crushed ice 1-2 tsp caramelized, sugar for top coating

Preparation

Take a blender and blend the pumpkin pulp, sugar, cream, salt, crushed ice, and condensed milk. Make a thick paste, but do not use water directly. Take a round bottomed glass, and pour the smoothie into it. Garnish with a top coating of caramelized sugar, apricot kernels. Serve chilled Enjoy!

Lemon and Yogurt Smoothie

Ingredients

1 cup yogurt
½ cup raspberry juice
1 tsp berry syrup
2 tsp castor sugar
2 tsp fresh lemon juice

2 tsp sweet lemon pulp
    (sieved and deseeded)
¼ cup nuts
Mint leaves

Preparation

Add yogurt, nuts, raspberry and lemon pulp into the blender and blend it into a thick paste. Pour it into a glass, drizzle raspberry syrup, and garnish with lemon juice, mint leaves and nuts. Enjoy!

Lentil-Cashew nut Smoothie

Ingredients

½ cup lentil, soaked in milk for 5 hours
2-3 tsp refined sugar
Salt to taste

¼ cup Wafer biscuits
¼ cup cashew nuts, grated 1 cup yogurt

Preparation

Add lentils, sugar, salt and yogurt in the blender and blend it very well. Do not pour any water or crushed ice. The yogurt should be completely chilled. Pour the mixture in a tall glass in garnish it with grated cashew nuts, and wafer biscuits. Enjoy!

Avocado Rose Smoothie

Ingredients

1 cup avocado pulp
½ cup refined brown sugar granules
1 cup double toned milk
1/3 cup fresh cream 1 tsp salt
¼ cup Rose petals
Rose syrup for garnishing

Preparation

Add the avocado pulp, sugar, milk, salt, and Rose petals in a blender, and blend well for 3 minutes till it becomes a smooth paste. Pour it in a long-stemmed glass, and garnish with rose syrup and Rose petals. Add ice cubes and serve chilled. Enjoy!

Pink Delight

Ingredients

½ cup strawberries
1 tsp strawberry essence
½ cup water
1 cup condensed milk
1 cup crushed ice
2 tsp sugar
1 cup crushed strawberries, or strawberry pulp
2-3 tsp nuts and caramelized sugar for topping

Preparation

Blend strawberries, sugar, water condensed milk in a blender, and make a smooth paste. Fill half of a glass with this mixture, and put a thick layer of strawberry pulp on top. Then take condensed milk and fill the rest of the glass with it. Pour some more grated strawberry on top, and make a thick layer with crushed ice, nuts and caramelized sugar. Serve chilled. Enjoy!

Pomegranate-Chocolate Smoothie

Ingredients

½ cup grated dark chocolate
2 dark chocolate wedges
1 cup pomegranate
½ cup condensed milk
2 tsp refined sugar
2 tsp cashew nuts
2 tsp dried raisins
1 cup crushed ice
Chocolate sauce for garnishing

Preparation

Add pomegranate, dark chocolate. salt, refined sugar, raisins, cashew nuts, crushed ice and condensed milk in the blender and blend well. Fill more than half of a glass with this mixture. Fill the rest with chocolate sauce. Garnish with grated chocolate, raisins, and crushed ice. Serve it chilled Enjoy!

Turmeric Yogurt Smoothie

Ingredients

1 cup yogurt 1 tsp turmeric
1 tsp turmeric juice
½ cup refined castor sugar

½ cup crushed ice
½ cup protein supplements 1 Vitamin E capsule
Rose petals for garnishing

Preparation

Blend the yogurt, sugar, vitamin capsule and protein supplement and ice into a blender, and add the turmeric juice or the extract to it. Add Rose petals for garnishing. Serve chilled. Enjoy!

Yogurt Beetroot Smoothie

Ingredients

2 tsp red wine
2 tsp brown sugar (refined), grained
1 tsp salt
½ cup crushed ice

1 cup white soda
½ cup beet extracts
Mint leaves for garnishing

Preparation

Pour some wine in a glass. Put it in the freezer and let it chill for 2 hours. Then blend all the ingredients in the blender, except crushed ice. Pour the smoothie into the glass. Garnish with a mild wine shot, and grated beet. and mint leaves. Enjoy!

Triple Delight Smoothie

Ingredients

½ cup strawberry crushed
1 tsp strawberry syrup
½ cup mango pulp
1 tsp mango juice

2 tsp cashew nuts for garnishing
2 tsp chocolate syrup
2 tsp sugar granules
Chocolate sauce for topping

Preparation

First, blend the strawberry pulp with sugar and ice; fill 1/3rd of a glass with it. Add the strawberry syrup on top. Then blend mango pulp with sugar and pour over the remaining ½ portion of the glass to make a second layer. Finally, drizzle chocolate sauce and garnish with nuts. Enjoy!

Mixed Fruit Smoothie

Ingredients

½ cup each Jackfruit/mango/fruit beer/ blueberry
½ cup ice cubes
2-3 tsp brown sugar granules
1 tsp salt
2 tsp fresh cream
½ cup yogurt Mint leaves for garnishing
Pepper powder to sprinkle on top
You can also use vanilla essence or vanilla extract for an awesome taste

Preparation

First blend the deseeded jackfruit, blueberries, mango in a blender. Add cream, sugar, ice cubes and salt, and make a thick smoothie. Pour it in a tall-stemmed glass, and make another layer with yogurt mixed with vanilla essence. Pour this as a second layer. Garnish with mint leaves and pepper powder. Enjoy!

Custard apple Smoothie

Ingredients

2 cups custard apple
¼ cup sugar 1/3rd cup
1 ½ cup yogurt
5-6 mint leaves
1 tsp fresh basil paste
Chocolate wafers to garnish
½ cup barley boiled

Preparation

First, custard apple with yogurt and fill half of a round glass. Now pour yogurt blended with basil paste and sugar. Then make a topping with barley. Half-dip the wafers in it. Enjoy!

Espresso Smoothie with Cream and Chocolate

Ingredients

1/3 cup dark chocolate grated
2 tsp chocolate sauce
½ cup crushed ice
2 tsp coffee powder
2 tsp brown sugar
2 tsp chocolate essence

Preparation

Brew coffee and allow it to cool, refrigerate it for about 30 minutes. Pour the drink in a long-stemmed glass, and add chocolate sauce, cream, ice, brown sugar, and dark chocolate. Garnish with a layer of grated chocolate Enjoy!

Sizzling Smoothie

Ingredients

½ cup orange flavored soda
1 tsp orange extracts or essence
2 scoops butterscotch ice cream
2 tsp pistachio or apricot kernel grated
5-6 mint leaves
lemon rings for garnishing
1 cup Fresh and ultra-mild French White wine

Preparation

Blend the soda with sugar, pistachio, mint leaves and orange extracts in a blender and pour it into a large wine glass. Add ice cream scoops on it and pour white wine on top. garnish with lemon rings. Enjoy!

Multicoloured Smoothie

Ingredients

1 ½ cup chilled mixed fruits (mango, banana, pineapple, and grapes)
1 cup fresh yogurt
¼ cup cream, no fat
2 tsp brown sugar granules
Some basil leaves
1 cup crushed ice
Mango wedge or shredded pineapple for garnishing

Preparation

First blend each fruit individually and pour in a tall glass making an individual layer. Garnish with crushed ice, pineapple and basil leaves Enjoy!

Yellow Sunshine Smoothie

Ingredients

½ cup raw papaya, grated, boiled and caramelized with brown sugar
½ cup ripe papaya
2 tsp lemon essence
1 tsp refined white sugar
½ cup fresh mango-flavored yogurt
1 tsp edible food color (orange or yellow)
1 scoop vanilla ice cream

Preparation

Blend caramelized with sugar, food color, yogurt, and lemon essence. Make a smooth paste, and pour it into a glass. Fill half of the glass. Then blend the ripe Papaya and pour it as a top layer. Garnish with ice cream and lemon essence Enjoy!

Health Smoothie Ingredients

Ingredients
1 cup shredded cabbage (green or purple)
1 cup oats, cooked
1 tsp protein- shake 2 tsp brown sugar pellets
Fruits for garnishing (any)
1 tsp milk powder

Preparation
Combine all ingredients in a blender and form a thick smooth paste, serve chilled and garnish with fruits of choice. Enjoy!

Biscuit Smoothie

Ingredients
1 bowl Cream biscuits, crushed (lemon, orange and chocolate flavour)
½ cup oats, cooked
2 tsp refined brown sugar
1 cup crushed ice
2 cups watermelon (de-seeded and cut into wedges)
1 cup white soda. (use yogurt if you do not prefer soda)
1 tap watermelon essence
1 tsp vanilla extract
1 tsp salt

Preparation
Combine all ingredients in a blender until it forms a smooth creamy paste. Serve chilled. Enjoy!

Potato Baby-corn Smoothie

Ingredients
2 potatoes. (boiled, peel off the skin after boiling)
2 tsp sugar
2 tsp fresh cream
1 cup baby-corn (boiled and mashed)
2-3 tsp chocolate sauce
1-2 tsp chocolate chips
1 cup yogurt
1 tsp vanilla essence

Preparation
Blend the potatoes with sugar, cream, vanilla essence, chocolate sauce, and yogurt. Pour glass. Add a layer of yogurt mixed with boiled corn. Then garnish with fresh cream, vanilla essence, and chocolate chips. You can also dip wafer sticks into it. Enjoy!

Hale and Hearty Ginger-Banana Smoothie

Ingredients
1 tsp honey
1/3 tsp freshly grated ginger
1 banana, sliced
oz. vanilla yogurt

Preparation
Combine the yogurt, banana, ginger, honey. Add these ingredients to your mixer blender. Blend for 15 minutes. Increase the speed the blender gradually. You can add few ice cubes if desired. Leave the smoothie for 10 minutes for a good blend. Your smoothie is ready. Enjoy!

Kiwi and Strawberry Smoothie

Ingredients
1 ½ kiwi fruit, sliced
1 cup strawberries, frozen
2 tsp honey
1 ½ cup apple juice, chilled
1 ½ ripe banana, sliced

Preparation
Blend the sliced banana, kiwifruit, honey, and apple juice. Add these ingredients in the mixer. Add ice cubes if desired. Enjoy!

Avocado Smoothie

Ingredients
1 ½ cups ice cubes
2 ripe avocados,
1 cup milk
1 cup sweetened condensed milk

Preparation
Add ice, milk, condensed milk (sweetened) to a blender. Blend the mixture until it becomes very smooth. Add in the avocado pulp to the mixture and blend the mixture again. Now. add chilled water to the mixture. Blend it again to make the mixture thin. You can add the condensed milk if you want to make it more sweetened. Blend the smoothie until it becomes smooth. The smoothie is ready to be served. Enjoy!

Raspberry Smoothies

Ingredients

1/3 cup freshly squeezed orange juice
1/3 cup skimmed milk
1/3 cup yogurt, Greek or regular
1 cups ice
1 ripe banana
4 fresh raspberries
1 tablespoon honey

Preparation

Add raspberries, banana, milk, banana, orange juice, yogurt, ice to a blender. Blend until they become smooth. Serve chilled. Enjoy!

Basil Smoothie

Ingredients

2 tsp lemon syrup
1 cup water
1 cup fresh basil leaves
1 cup sugar
1 tsp lemon zest
1 cup plain yogurt
1 cup ice cubes

Preparation:

To prepare lemon syrup, add water, lemon zest in a saucepan. Stir occasionally until the sugar gets dissolved. Remove the pan from heat and leave the syrup to cool, about 15 minutes.
Blend yogurt, basil, and lemon Syrup, and ice cubes. Mix together until smooth and foamy. Pour into chilled glasses and serve immediately. Enjoy!

Banana - Papaya Smoothie

Ingredients

1 small ripe banana,
2 cups ripe papaya, peeled, de-seeded, peeled and chopped
1 cup ice cubes
1 tsp vanilla extract
1 ½ cup milk
½ cup yogurt

Preparation

Add banana, ripe papaya, milk, yogurt, ice cubes to a blender. Blend the ingredients until those are mixed thoroughly. You can add ice cubes if desired. Serve. Enjoy!

Pumpkin Smoothie

Ingredients

1/3 cup vanilla yogurt
1/3 tsp cinnamon
1/3 cup cinnamon graham cracker crumbs

14-ounces canned pumpkin pie filling
2 cups milk

Preparation

Put the pumpkin pie filling into the muffin cups. Cover the pan with aluminium foil and place it in a freezer. Combine milk, yogurt, and cinnamon in a blender. Add 4 pieces of the frozen pumpkin pie to the mixture. Blend the mixture until it becomes smooth. The smoothie is ready. Garnish the smoothie with graham cracker crumbs before serving. Pour the smoothie into chilled glasses serve it with straw. Enjoy!

Mango Smoothie

Ingredients

1 cup peaches frozen
1/3 block soft tofu
1 cup ice cubes
2 ounces vanilla vodka

1 cup mango nectar
7-ounce peach yogurt
1 cup mango frozen

Preparation

Add mango nectar, frozen peaches, soft smooth tofu, ice cubes, peach yogurt, and frozen mango in a blender. Blend until it becomes smooth. Once the smoothie is ready, add 2 ounces vanilla vodka if Serve Chilled Enjoy!

Summer Day Smoothie

Ingredients

2 mangoes, chopped
15-ounce strawberries,
15-ounce peaches

7-ounce guava nectar
2 tsp fresh strawberries, for garnishing

Preparation

Combine all ingredients and blend until smooth, serve chilled and garnish with strawberries. Enjoy!

Raspberry Vanilla Smoothie

Ingredients

½ cup water
1 cup frozen raspberries
1 tsp vanilla extract
2 cups ice cubes

½ cup apple juice
1 cup plain yogurt
½ cup sugar

Preparation

Add sugar and water to a saucepan and boil, Stir occasionally over low heat until the sugar is dissolved. Remove from heat and let it cool. Pour the syrup in a blender along with apple juice, vanilla extract, ice cubes, raspberries and yogurt And blend until smooth. Pour into chilled glasses and serve. Enjoy!

Purple Grape Smoothie

Ingredients

1 ½ cup yogurt
1 ½ cup milk
2 ½ tablespoons honey
½ cup ice cubes

1 ½ cup purple grapes
1 cup strawberries
1 ripe banana
1 cup blueberries

Preparation

Combine all ingredients in a blender until smooth. Serve chilled. Enjoy!

Smoothie with Berries

Ingredients

2 cups almond milk, chilled
½ cup fresh mango, chopped
1/3 medium banana, peeled and cut into large pieces

1/3 cup blueberries, frozen
½ cup strawberries, frozen

Preparation:

Combine all ingredients in a blender until smooth. Serve chilled. Enjoy!

Melon Smoothie

Ingredients

1 ½ cup vanilla yogurt, low fat
2 cups honeydew melon, de-seeded and chopped
1 juice of lime
1 ½ cup ice cubes
2 cups watermelon, chopped

Preparation:

Blend vanilla yogurt, honeydew melon, lime juice, watermelon, and ice in a blender. Serve chilled. Enjoy!

Blueberry Smoothie

Ingredients

1 tsp honey
½ cup plain yogurt
1 cup blueberries, frozen - preferably unsweetened
1/3 cup milk, low fat

Preparation:

Combine all the ingredients in a blender until smooth. Serve chilled. Enjoy!

Vanilla Coconut Smoothie

Ingredients

2 ½ cups yogurt
1 ½ cup coconut water, frozen in an ice cube tray
1/3 cup honey
1 vanilla bean, split laterally
1 ½ tsp fresh mint leaves, for garnishing

Preparation

Add the honey, vanilla bean and water in a saucepan. Bring them to boil. Stir it occasionally for 7 minutes on low heat. Allow the mixture to cool at room temperature. The mixture and frozen cube of coconut water in a blender. Blend for around a minute The Smoothie is ready to be served. Enjoy!

Fresh Morning Smoothie

Ingredients

½ cup bananas
1 cup baby spinach
½ tablespoon honey
1 ½ tsp vanilla extract
1 cup whole oats

1 1/3 cups peaches or mango, chopped
1 cup ice cubes
1 cup milk (vanilla almond, coconut or soy)

Preparation

Blend oats and milk in a blender. Now blend the remaining ingredients until smooth. Serve chilled. Enjoy!

Fruit and Spice Smoothie

Ingredients

1 cup Greek yogurt
1 cup bananas, chopped
1 cup mango, chopped
2 cups peaches, cored

1 tbs honey
¼ tbs nutmeg powder
1/3 cup ice cubes
2-3 mint leaves, for garnish

Preparation

Blend Greek yogurt, bananas, mango, peaches, honey, nutmeg powder, and ice cubes in a blender, until smooth. Pour the smoothie in tall glasses and garnish with mint leaves. You may want to add some chopped mangoes to the blended mix while serving, for a slushy feel. Serve chilled. Enjoy!

Spiced Cream n' Pumpkin Smoothie

Ingredients

1 cup pumpkin puree
1 cup almond/vanilla milk, or regular milk
¼ tbs nutmeg powder
2-3 tbs almonds, roasted and coarsely chopped
¼ tbs cinnamon powder

½ tbs ginger root, peeled and grated
1 tsp salt
¼ cup pumpkin, grated, chopped or diced (optional) for a crunchy texture
½ cup ice cubes
2-3 mint leaves, for garnish

Preparation

Combine pumpkin puree, almond milk, nutmeg powder, ginger, ice cubes, and salt in a blender until it forms an orange, creamy texture. Now pour the blended mix in a tall glass and add roasted almonds and cinnamon powder to the mix, stir well. Add chopped pumpkin if you want to bite into each diced chunk. Sprinkle a dash of nutmeg powder and cinnamon powder on top and garnish with mint leaves. Serve chilled. Enjoy!

Banana-Almond Milk Smoothie

Ingredients

2 bananas, chopped
1 cup almond milk
½ tbs vanilla essence or vanilla extract
½ tbs cocoa powder
½ tbs powdered Peanut Butter
¼ cup almonds, roasted and coarsely chopped
½ cup ice cubes
1-2 tsp Chia seeds (optional for topping)
A dash of cinnamon powder, for garnishing

Preparation

Blend almond milk, chopped bananas, vanilla essence, cocoa powder, and ice cubes until smooth. Pour the drink in a tall glass and add roasted chopped almonds and stir, now generously top it up with chia seeds and dust cinnamon powder. Serve chilled. Enjoy!

Peanut Butter and Fruit Jelly Smoothie

Ingredients

1 ½ cup soy milk
2 bananas
1 tbs creamy peanut butter
1 tsp wheat germ or flax seeds
2 ½ tbs Strawberries/Raspberries/Blueberries jelly
1 cup ice cubes
2 tbs brown sugar or honey, (optional)

Preparation

Blend soymilk, bananas, creamy peanut butter, fruit jelly, and honey in a blender until it forms a smooth past like texture. Now add ice cubes and wheat germ and blend coarsely for a few seconds, make sure you do not over do it. Now pour the smoothie in chilled glasses and serve. Enjoy!

Banana- Ginger Smoothie

Ingredients

2 bananas
½ tbs fresh ginger root, peeled and grated
2 tbs brown sugar or honey, (optional)
1 cup ice cubes
1 cup flavored yogurt

Preparation

Combine bananas, fresh grated ginger, brown sugar, ice cubes and yogurt in a blender until it forms a creamy and smooth consistency. Pour the blended mix in tall glasses and serve chilled. If you do not like the natural taste of fresh ginger, you may use concentrated ginger extract. Enjoy!

Orange-Nutmeg Dream Creamsicle

Ingredients

1 navel oranges, peeled and de-seeded
2 tbs orange concentrate, frozen preferred
1 tsp vanilla bean extract or vanilla essence
½ cup ice cubes
½ cup yogurt, fat free
1 tbs vodka or brandy, optional

Preparation

Blend navel oranges, frozen orange concentrate, vanilla bean extract, ice cubes, and fat free yogurt until smooth. You may add vodka while blending the smoothie or, pour the drink in glasses and choose you flambé the finished product with vodka or brandy for a crisp bittersweet after taste. Enjoy!

Green Tea and Banana Berry Smoothie

Ingredients

½ cup water
1 green tea bag
1-2 tbs honey
1 tsp frozen concentrated ginger extract, optional
1 cup blue berries, frozen
½ cup bananas, frozen and chopped
½ cup vanilla flavored milk
5-6 ice cubes

Preparation

Boil water in a pot until steaming hot and remove the pot from heat. Now add green tea bag and brew it for 3-4 minutes. Remove the tea bag, add honey to the tea, and stir until it dissolves. Allow it to cool at room temperature. Combine brewed green tea, frozen ginger concentrate, blue berries, bananas, and vanilla flavored milk with ice cubes until smooth. Remove the mix in glasses and serve chilled. Enjoy!

Dry Fruit Smoothie

Ingredients

1 cup vanilla flavored milk, chilled
3-4 tbs brown sugar
3 tbs almonds, chopped
3 tbs cashew nuts, chopped
3 tbs pistachios, chopped (unsalted)
2-3 tbs walnuts, chopped
2 dates, (cored, chopped and soaked in vanilla milk for 30 minutes)
2 tbs dried apricots, chopped
2 tbs dried figs, chopped
¼ tbs pepper powder
½ tbs nutmeg, grated
1 tbs honey, for garnishing

Preparation

Combine vanilla flavored milk with brown sugar, chopped almonds, cashew nuts pistachios, walnuts, dates, apricots, figs, pepper powder, and grated nutmeg until they blend well. Pour the drink in chilled glasses and drizzle honey on top. Serve chilled. Enjoy!

Pineapple Passion Smoothie

Ingredients

2 cups canned pineapples, discard the syrup
1 ½ cup vanilla yogurt
1 cup ice cubes
2-3 tbs sweetened cherries, cored and chopped

Preparation

Blend pineapples, vanilla yogurt, ice cubes until a smooth consistency is achieved. Pour the drink in chilled glasses, add sweetened cherries, and stir well. Serve chilled. Enjoy!

Valentine's Smoothie

Ingredients

1 cup strawberries, fresh and chopped
2 cups apple juice, chilled
1 cup kiwi, peeled and chopped
½ tsp cinnamon powder
2 scoops vanilla ice cream
2 tbs honey
2 tbs dark chocolate, grated

Preparation

Blend strawberries, apple juice, kiwifruit, and cinnamon powder until smooth. Pour the drink in two chilled glasses and add vanilla ice cream. Drizzle honey and sprinkle grated dark chocolate over it. Serve immediately. Enjoy!

Cucumber Smoothie

Ingredients

2 large cucumbers, peeled and chopped (preferably chilled)
¼ tbs rock salt
1 sprig fresh celery, chopped
¼ cup mint leaves

Preparation

Blend cucumbers, rock salt, chopped celery, and mint leaves until it turns into a green liquid. Pour in chilled glasses, garnish with mint leaves, and serve chilled. Enjoy!

Tomato-Basil Smoothie

Ingredients

8-10 large tomatoes, chopped
1 small radish, peeled and chopped
1 sprig mint leaves
¼ tbs salt
¼ tbs black pepper powder
5-6 basil leaves
1 juice of lime
½ cup ice cubes

Preparation

Blend tomatoes, radish, mint leaves, salt, black pepper, lime juice and ice cubes until smooth. Add basil leaves and blend for just about two seconds. You may use fresh peppercorns instead of black pepper powder if you prefer a spicy taste. Pour the smoothie in tall chilled glasses, garnish with mint leaves, and serve chilled. Enjoy!

Tropical Fusion Smoothie

Ingredients

1 cup pineapple, chopped
½ cup ripe papaya, chopped
1 tbs coconut extract
1 cup yogurt, fat free
½ cup ice cubes
2 tbs white rum, optional
2 tbs fresh cream
1 tbs flax seeds, crushed

Preparation

Combine pineapples, ripe papaya, coconut extract, yogurt, ice cubes, and white rum in a blender until smooth and frosty. Pour the drink in chilled glasses, garnish with fresh cream, and crushed flax seeds. Enjoy!

Peach Smoothie

Ingredients

1 cup soy milk
1 cup vanilla yogurt, low fat
½ cup peaches, frozen
½ cup strawberries, fresh
¼ tbs ginger powder, optional
1 ½ whey protein powder
5-6 ice cubes
½ cup oats, cooked
2 tbs honey

Preparation

Combine soymilk, frozen peaches, strawberries, ginger powder and whey protein and blend until the grainy powder is evenly blended. Now, add ice cubes, cooked oats, and thoroughly blend until it forms a thick consistency. Pour the smoothie in chilled glasses, drizzle honey over it, and serve chilled Enjoy!

Tutti-Fruity Smoothie

Ingredients

½ cup loose-pack mixed berries, frozen
¼ cup strawberries
¼ cup black grapes, frozen
1 ripe banana, chopped
½ cup canned pineapple juice
½ cup orange juice, optional
1 cup yogurt, low fat
5-6 ice cubes

Preparation

Blend loose-packed mixed berries, strawberries, black grapes, frozen black grapes, banana, canned pineapple juice, orange juice and low fat yogurt and blend until frosty. Now add ice cubes in a glass and pour the smoothie in it. Serve chilled. Enjoy!

Banana-Soy Smoothie

Ingredients

2 ripe bananas, chopped
¼ cup almonds, roasted and chopped
¼ cup dry figs, chopped
2 tbs honey
1 cup soymilk
¼ cup crushed digestive biscuits (or cooked oats)
1 tsp vanilla bean extract
5-6 ice cubes, optional

Preparation

Combine bananas, almonds, dry figs, honey, soymilk, crushed digestive biscuits, vanilla bean extract and ice cubes in a blender until smooth. Pour in chilled glasses and serve. Enjoy!

Carrot-Celery Smoothie

Ingredients

1 cup carrots, grated
½ cup celery stalks, chopped
1 tbs lime juice
¼ tsp salt, optional
1 cup Greek yogurt
1 cup ice cubes
3-4 mint leaves

Preparation

Blend grated carrots, celery stalks, lime juice, salt, Greek yogurt, and ice cube until it forms a smooth orange puree. Serve in tall chilled glasses and garnish with mint leaves. Enjoy!

Rose Smoothie

Ingredients

1 cup milk, low fat
2-3 tbs rose syrup
2 tbs sugar
1 cup ice cubes

¼ cup rice vermicelli, pre-cooked
2 tbs almonds, fine chopped
Tender red rose petals for garnishing, optional

Preparation

Blend milk, rose syrup, sugar and ice cubes thoroughly. Now, add pre-cooked vermicelli in two tall glasses, pour the pink liquid over it and add fine chopped almonds, rose petals and serve chilled. Enjoy!

Marshmallow Smoothie

Ingredients

1 cup marshmallows
1 kiwi, peeled and chopped

2 tbs honey
1 cup ice cubes

Preparation

Combine marshmallow, honey and ice cubes in a blender until a rich creamy textures is achieved. Take two tall chilled glasses and fill them with chopped kiwi equally, pour the blend over it and stir. Serve chilled. Enjoy!

Evil-Eye Smoothie

Ingredients

1 cup banana, chopped
1 large avocado, peeled, cored and chopped
1 cucumber, peeled and chopped

½ cup broccoli florets
2 tbs lime juice
1 cup yogurt, low fat
1 cup ice cubes

Preparation

Combine banana, avocado, cucumber, broccoli florets, lime juice, yogurt and ice cubes in a blender until a pale green smooth texture is achieved. Pour in chilled glasses and serve immediately. Enjoy!

Bottle Gourd Smoothie

Ingredients

1 cup bottle gourd
1 cup yogurt
1 cup cucumber

½ cup silken tofu
¼ cup mint leaves
5-6 ice cubes

Preparation

Blend bottle gourd, yogurt, cucumber, silken tofu, mint leaves, and ice cubes until it turns into a light green smoothie. Pour the drink in tall chilled glasses and serve immediately. Enjoy!

Cherry-Lime-Basil Smoothie

Ingredients

1 ½ cups cherries, frozen
1 cup milk, low fat
1 tbs lime juice

¼ cup mint leaves
1 sprig basil leaves
5-6 ice cubes

Preparation

Blend frozen cherries, milk, limejuice, mint leaves, basil leaves, and ice cubes until frosty. Pour the mixture in chilled tall glasses and serve immediately. Enjoy!

Ginger-Apple Smoothie

Ingredients

2 large green apples, de-seeded and chopped (do not peel)
1 tbs concentrated ginger syrup
¼ tbs cinnamon powder
2 tbs honey

1 sprig parsley leaves, chopped
1 cup club soda, chilled
½ cup crushed ice
¼ cup tbs white rum, optional
3-4 mint leaves, for garnishing

Preparation

Blend apples, ginger syrup, cinnamon powder, honey, parsley, and club soda, until smooth. Take two tall glasses and add crushed ice in them equally. Pour white rum and add the blended concoction over it. Garnish with mint leaves and serve chilled. Enjoy!

Raspberry-Rosemary Smoothie

Ingredients

2 tbs concentrated raspberry syrup or (1 cup frozen raspberries)
1 fresh sprig rosemary, chopped
½ cup Greek yogurt
½ cup ice cubes

Preparation

Combine concentrated raspberry syrup, fresh chopped rosemary, Greek yogurt, and ice cubes in a blender until it turns frosty. Pour the mixture in tall frozen glasses and serve chilled. Enjoy!

Cilantro Smoothie

Ingredients

1 Sprig fresh cilantro, chopped
1 tbs lime juice
6-8 mint leaves
1 cup Greek yogurt

Preparation

Blend fresh chopped cilantro, limejuice, mint leaves, and Greek yogurt until it turns into a pale green smoothie. Pour in chilled tall glasses and serve chilled. Garnish with mint leaves. Enjoy!

Raw Mango Smoothie

Ingredients

4 raw mangoes, boiled, peeled and pureed
1 ½ cup sugar
2 cups ice cubes
½ tbs rock salt
1 sprig mint leaves, chopped
2 cups chilled water

Preparation

Use a pressure cooker, add raw mangoes (do not peel skin yet) for 15 minutes. Allow them to cool at room temperature. Peel the skin and mash the mangoes, discard the seed. In a blender, add the boiled raw mango pulp, sugar, ice cubes, rock salt, and mint leaves until it forms a smooth texture. Take two glasses and pour half the glass with pureed raw mango mix and the rest of the glass with chilled water. Stir well. Garnish with mint leaves. Serve chilled. Enjoy!

Veggie-Delight Smoothie

Ingredients

2 large tomatoes, chopped
1 large beetroot, chopped
1 large carrot, peeled and chopped
1 cup fresh mint leaves, chopped
1 cup fresh parsley leaves, chopped
¼ tbs cayenne pepper

1-2 tbs lime juice
¼ tbs salt
½ tbs freshly crushed peppercorns
1 cup Greek yogurt
1 tsp lemon zest, for garnishing

Preparation

Combine chopped tomatoes, beets, carrots, mint, parsley, cayenne pepper, lime juice, salt, pepper powder, and Greek yogurt in a blender until the texture turns silky-smooth. Pour the mixture in chilled glasses, garnish with fresh mint leaves, lemon zest, and serve. Enjoy!

Custard-apple Smoothie

Ingredients

2 cups custard apples, fresh, peeled, de-seeded
1 large banana
2 tbs honey
1 cup vanilla flavored milk

¼ tbs cardamom powder
A pinch of grated nutmeg
¼ cup roasted almonds, coarsely chopped
1 tsp vanilla bean extract
1 cup ice cubes

Preparation

Combine custard apples, banana, honey, vanilla flavored milk, cardamom powder, grated nutmeg, vanilla bean extract and ice cubes in a blender until it forms a silky-smooth white creamy texture. Pour the mixture in tall chilled glasses, add coarsely chopped roasted almonds, and stir well. Serve chilled. Enjoy!

Cranberry Smoothie

Ingredients

1 cup cranberry juice, chilled
1 cup fresh cranberries
1 ½ cup canned pineapples, chopped, discard the syrup
4 tbs white rum

1 cup silken tofu
1 cup ice cubes
2 tbs coconut cream
Some orange rind for garnishing

Preparation

Combine cranberry juice, fresh cranberries, chopped canned pineapples, white rum, silken tofu, and ice cubes in a blender until smooth. Pour the mixture in tall chilled glasses and garnish with coconut cream and orange rind. Serve immediately. Enjoy!

Sapodilla- Coco Smoothie

Ingredients

2 ½ cups milk, low fat
2 cups sapodilla, peeled and cored and chopped
1 cup ice cubes
1 cup sugar
1 tbs coco powder

Preparation

Combine milk, chopped sapodilla, ice cubes, sugar, and coco powder in a blender to form a thick paste. Pour the mixture in tall chilled glassed and serve. Enjoy!

Conclusion

Everyone enjoys a glass of smoothie. There are 365 recipes in this book, which makes it easier for you to choose your favourite smoothies. Pick the ones that you find interesting
I hope that your journey of smoothies will be a great one ahead.
Thanks

Thank you again for purchasing this book!

Finally, if you enjoyed this book, please take the time to share your thoughts and post a review on Amazon. It'd be greatly appreciated!

Feel free to contact me at emma.katie@outlook.com

Check out more books by Emma Katie at:

www.amazon.com/author/emmakatie

Made in the USA
Lexington, KY
20 November 2018